# The Normal
# The Deep
and The
# Crazy

# THE NORMAL

# THE DEEP

# AND

# THE CRAZY

By

CATHERINE BROWN

JUST PUBLISHING

First published 2003

Unless otherwise indicated, Biblical quotations are from
the New International Version © 1973, 1978, 1984
by The International Bible Society

ISBN 0-9740554-0-9


Published by Just Publishing
408 Pacific Oaks Road
Goleta, CA 93117
USA

## DEDICATIONS

I want to dedicate this book to three groups of people:

To my minister, Rev D Ross Mitchell, and to other dear pastors and leaders who have embraced me into their midst across the nations, I thank you for your faithfulness, loyalty and trustworthiness to see this 'rough diamond' come right for Christ. I appreciate all that you have done for me individually and collectively to help me fulfil my God given destiny. A special mention to YWAM for facilitating life changing encounters where I met with the living God.

To my friends, young and old, who carried and cared for me when I was too tired to go on and who laughed with me through the good times and wept with me during the tough times. You know who you are, and I dedicate this book to all of you – you helped to make it happen.

And last, but not least, I dedicate this book to my loving family – every single one of them. You mean everything to me and I would be lost without your love.

'To live is Christ, to die is gain'.

# ACKNOWLEDGMENTS

I would like to personally thank my husband Stephen for his magnificent love and patience as this book has been written and re-written. It's been a rollercoaster ride that I couldn't have made without his solid devotion to Christ and his commitment to our marriage. At the outset of writing this book, Stephen said a most prophetic statement, which is at the heart of 'The normal, the deep and the crazy'. He quietly stated, 'it's not just a book, it's a Kingdom event'. We were blown away by the simplicity, power and purity of those words.

Our children, Mark, Daniel, Rebecca and Samuel have been wee stars, allowing mum to do what Jesus asked of her, which sometimes meant I had to spend intense periods of time at the computer or working on the manuscript by hand, during the different seasons of the writing and editing process. Thanks kids. I love you infinity.

We would also like to express our appreciation to all our friends and family on both sides of the Atlantic who have encouraged us, believed in us and donated financially and prayerfully to the book, with a special note of gratitude to David Plews for a significant financial gift. For those who've written the endorsements for this publication a special thank you.

Thank you my heavenly Father for loving me as your daughter; thank you my Lord Jesus for saving me from sin and healing my broken heart; and thank you Holy Spirit for being my best friend and constant Source of creativity and inspiration. Lord, let this book be a 'Kingdom Event' as Stephen spoke out in faith! Let your Kingdom come here on earth , as it is in heaven.

Lovingly,

Catherine

## ENDORSEMENTS

I have no hesitation in commending both Catherine and her ministry to you. On the personal level Catherine is a mature Christian of genuine commitment. She is humble and has shown a consistent desire to be accountable in all aspects of her ministry. I have been in ministry for 20 years, and I consider her heart to be attuned to the Lord in terms of the prophetic and in terms of intercession. I regard her highly in terms of the accuracy of her hearing, and consider her to be a forerunner in terms of what God is doing in the land - not an easy place to be. I have ministered with Catherine and saw the blessing that attended what she said and the way she said it. I would warmly commend her to you.

**Rev. Kenny Borthwick**
Church of Scotland minister, and leader of New Wine, Scotland.

Catherine's openness and vulnerability in sharing her prophetic journey in The Normal, The Deep and The Crazy will warm your heart and bring great encouragement. Through her personal testimony, you will find that she paints a beautiful picture and profile of the character and gifting that is required to shape a prophetic vessel, fit for the Master's use. This book will enable many to rise up in courage to embrace the high calling of Christ that resides within them.

**Pat Cocking**
President  Christian Services Association, Canada
**www.the-war-room.com**

I've known Catherine for a while now, and we've shared good times and bad. I would encourage you to read this book. It is incredibly open and if you've ever felt, "Have only I experienced this?" then you should read it. I know you'll be encouraged, inspired, challenged and uplifted by this awesome testimony.

**Your  wee Sarah 17**

We have come to know Catherine over the last year and found her purity, prophetic gifting, and personality to be a precious refreshing gift from God. Her ability to hear from God and interpret what He is saying into situations and lives we have found remarkably accurate. We recommend her for ministry, and look forward to hearing good reports from the fruit of it.

**Julie Anderson,**
Founder of Prayer for the Nations.

Catherine is a mother to many and has such a heart for this generation to see them released into their destiny and calling. I've been privileged to be mentored by such a precious woman of God. She has such fire for the Lord and passion for the lost. I've been blown away by some of our times of prayer and worship. These times will stay close to my heart forever.

**Mick Craig, 22**

For the past few years I've had the honour to have worked with and been mentored by one of this generation's radically passionate women of God, Catherine Brown. Catherine's life is truly inspiring. Her love for Christ is a beacon of hope in a dark, dying world. I pray that through reading this book you will get to know Catherine in the way I know and love her. This is a journey of truth, love and grace.

**Hugh Donald, 22**

Catherine Brown has been a friend and associate of our prophetic "Elijah List," from almost day one. She is one who hears from God and who speaks even into other lands. She has been used to connect many in the Body of Christ throughout the world. May the Lord continue to use her words to encourage the worldwide Church. She has been enlisted into God's army for such a time as this. I have known few from whom I sensed such a passion for Jesus Christ.

**Steve Shultz, Publisher**
THE ELIJAH LIST
www.elijahlist.com

# PREFACE

Unaccustomed as I am to being in the public gaze, I have somewhat reluctantly agreed to supply my dear wife with a preface. Apparently, a preface is a short introductory essay, preceding the text of a book. I am not allowed to write about my love of medieval history, or even Italian opera, so this preface will therefore be necessarily short.

I have asked my wife to restrain her hand, when describing events that I have been a party to. So, you should find my name mentioned in but a few places. This is because Catherine's book is about Catherine's journey, and her relationship with our Lord. I am inconsequential to this great scheme of events, like a small lifeboat being pulled behind an expensive yacht. I am in a very privileged position to see how Normal, Deep, or Crazy things can be around here. We stand together, my wife and I, and yet we are so different in many respects. Were I to write this same tale from my perspective it would make a dull book indeed. Therefore, I know in my faith that you will enjoy reading this book, and I sincerely hope that it will encourage and strengthen you in our commission.

Catherine's journey thus far, has been a rollercoaster. It is a tale that comes from the deprivation in our homeland here on the west coast of Scotland and leads to the manifest glory of God, new hope, and the broad new horizons of the future. Through a personal encounter with our Lord, and perhaps by reading this book, Catherine and I pray that you will have life, and have it to the fullest. Enjoy!

Stephen Brown

# FOREWARD

Written in an amazingly transparent style, Catherine Brown's book The Normal, The Deep and The Crazy adds a much needed gem to the prayer and prophetic movements in these days. I have had the joy of interacting with Catherine over the internet over the past few years and meeting her in person. I appreciate immensely her humility and genuine heart for Jesus.

Having been in the prayer and prophetic movement for several years myself, I look for clear voices that attempt to bring forth a word that honours the Lord and edifies and challenges the body of Christ. This is what I found in the ministry of Jesus through this clay vessel. Catherine Brown is a quick learner and humble servant. She is one of the new breed; a faceless generation of Esthers, Daniels, Josephs, and Deborahs whom the Lord is raising up to influence this Impact Generation.

With a whole heart I gladly endorse the content of this inspiring book. I trust it will do for you what it did for me. After reading The Normal, The Deep and The Crazy, I found myself more in love with our Father God who desires to see restoration happen in the lives of countless numbers of warriors–in–waiting. I sense the Holy Spirit saying, "Come out of your caves! I will embrace you! I will restore you! I will revive you! The best is yet ahead of you! Just as I have done in the life of this broken vessel - so I will I do for you!"

To you, the reader, I commend these telling truths from a pilgrim of faith. May the Lord impart to you the spirit of encouragement that all things are possible to those who believe! To you, Catherine, blessings, and, thank you.

Jim W. Goll
Co-founder of Ministry to the Nations, Franklin, TN
www.ministrytothenations.com

*Author of: The Lost Art of Intercession, Kneeling on the Promises, The Coming Prophetic Revolution, Exodus Cry, Intercession: The Power and the Passion to Shape History and Elijah's Revolution.*

# CONTENTS

# THE NORMAL

# THE DEEP

# AND

# THE CRAZY

# INTRODUCTION

This is my story, well, sort of. It's an end without a beginning and a beginning without an end. It isn't finished. It describes some of my childhood, the path I chose as a teenager that took me away from Jesus, and then my journey back as a young adult to God my Father. It's about the ravages of addiction, and how God rescued a worn down, battered young woman from hopelessness and a life style of deception. It's reality TV without the TV. It's about my Dad and I and touching heaven and breaking free from hell. It's passion and pain. It's fear and faith. It's rejection then acceptance. Above all it's about His love, that's the Source.

Who am I? I'm a thirty something, nameless, faceless, and a fore-runner with a message. So what's my message? My Dad has a Voice! I didn't always know that. At fifteen I believed in Jesus but I hadn't met my Father yet. Until I experienced God's Fatherly love, my heart was locked and my ears were blocked to the true sound of the Spirit. Even if I had been able to believe that God would speak to a 'nobody' like me, I would have expected thunderbolts and lightning and a loud judgemental voice. That isn't what I now know to be true.

I didn't really recognise the sound of God's voice until Jesus healed the many bruises on my soul. I cried a lot and he cared amazingly. I learned to trust God and I realised his heart is his voice. The warm compassion of my King unarmed me and melted this ice maiden's heart. It was the soft whisper of his love, and, his gentle understanding, that led me in. I was astonished that the God of all creation wanted to speak to 'wee me', in dreams and visions.

It seemed astonishing that he really cared enough to talk with me, and share his hopes and plans for people, nations and generations. The closer we've become, the more clearly I've been able to hear him. Who is this book for? This is for the little girl I used to be, the woman that I now am, and the person I have yet to become, and … it's for you. God wants all his children to experience his love and hear his Voice!

The Holy Spirit inspired me to write this book, and so did many friends. We've fallen on the floor together, our faces wet with tears from worship and prayer; we've danced, we've laughed, we've hoped, we've dreamed, we've run, we've fallen down again, and then, we've picked each other up and started over.

This is for Sarah (17), a high school student and servant-hearted worshipper, whose courage and faith in God have helped her to overcome rejection and abandonment. It's for Mick (22), a mad, way-too busy youth pastor and former clubber that God rescued from promiscuity and whose heart now burns with a pure and holy passion for revival. It's for Howard (23), youth worker and poet warrior who drums love songs to Jesus 24-7. It's for Stephen (22), post graduate science student, who has had more crazy hair colours and styles than I've had McDonald's, and loves those who don't know Jesus in a way that hurts. It's for Matthew (20), a Jewish Scot with the filthiest feet I've ever seen and loved because he walks barefoot for Jesus as a sacrifice of praise.

It's for Naomi (20), who found the Grace to carry on after her mum died tragically just a few years ago and is now a Christian drama/dance student who truly believes that the 'dry bones' can become an army. It's for Lindsay (20), waitress, who was miraculously healed from Alopecia, and now gives herself to serving orphans, drug addicts, homeless people and street girls.

It's for Hugh (22), an intercessor and prophet, healed from seven years of depression, he makes us all laugh and cry at the same time with his joy and wonder of the love of God at work in his life. It's for Simon (17) who is a sledgehammer with a guitar winning Goths for God – a new punk for the Prince of peace! It's for Jonathan (22), a business studies graduate, and young Irish prophet sold out in intimacy for Christ. It's for Charlene (20) the quiet, shy girl who threw away her inhibitions and trusted Jesus to do mission work. It's for Colin (21), young evangelist, who is nuts about sports and is currently praying his whole family into the kingdom (with major success). It's for Fraser (21) graffiti artist, following the Call. There are many more I could write about here but time and space dictate I move on. Maybe you recognise yourself?

So why read my story? Well, we might have more in common than you realise. My friends and I are extreme in our desperation for the 'more' of Jesus. Perhaps you, just like us, are longing for the day when actions will replace words in the arena of radical intimacy with Jesus. Our priority is relationship because we realise that is what the kingdom is all about. It's about lifestyle, and not language. It's about blessing and not bias. Passion in our Father's house is always relevant. If you believe that, then this book is for you. Get ready for a rollercoaster ride. This book will change your life because it's about a life that's been radically changed by God. I have written this book as if we were drinking tea or coffee in my kitchen, and sharing my journey. The style is casual and natural, with the occasional hint of the accent of Scotland. I hope you also hear the accents and sounds of Heaven. Open your heart to God, and listen to his voice.

# PART 1

# THE NORMAL

*Normal; adj. Conforming to a standard; usual, typical or expected'*

# CHAPTER 1

# WHO AM I?

I was an illegitimate child. Was I wanted? Yes, I think so. Was I an accident? Who am I? Why was I born? These questions, like sand in your eyes were a painful and uninvited source of irritation. I hated the b****** word. The children in our street used to call me names. It was painful to be mocked by them and it seared my soul with worthlessness. Even though my mum and dad had married by this time, it made no difference to the name-calling.

My dad was an alcoholic. Although he would never have admitted it, there was plenty of evidence to the contrary, especially in the destructive effects of his fists. If you were to ask me for a definition of normal, I don't know if I could easily answer you. The Oxford Dictionary states, 'normal; adj. Conforming to a standard; usual, typical or expected'. It was usual for my dad to get drunk; it was typical that he would become violent and it was expected that someone (usually my mum) would be seriously hurt as a result. This was the only home life I and my younger brother and sister knew, and therefore it was what we considered to be 'normal' as we were growing up.

Our family suffered deeply under the trauma of my dad's alcohol-induced violent outbursts. We moved around quite a bit because my parents were continually splitting up and then getting back together again. We lived on the dizzy merry go-round of impending divorce, whilst seesawing between the ecstatic emotion of reunion, and the dreadful depression of the 'normal' lifestyle recurring. We buried the brutal memories and tried to cope with our insecurities as best we could. It was like being on a storm-torn sea destined for a shipwreck.

## The bullying side of my Dad

I knew profound fear of my father – the kind that makes you wet the bed at night. He had an unnerving habit of sticking his face right into yours when he was angry. His mocking words were then snarled through clenched teeth. I had an extremely low self-esteem being the victim of frequent sarcastic remarks. I thought all dads were angry and authoritative.

Dad could also be given to sullen silences. He broke them usually in a gruff or aggressive manner. It was difficult not to be intimidated by him. He believed that children should be seen and not heard and eventually I believed that too. Not only did I feel silenced, but I also grew up experiencing the reality that my dad did not like talking to me very much and when he did, it often made me feel afraid.

Because we didn't talk much, I felt ignored. My dad wasn't very good at listening to me when I was little. Every Saturday his time was devoted to making bets on the racehorses and watching sports on television. There was no place for the children in dad's weekend routine.

Dad wasn't the hugging type. He would physically push me away each time I tried to get near to him. He liked his own space and would let you know when you were an unwelcome invader! Sadly, I have no memory of ever sitting on his knee except for the purpose of a photograph. Dad was just living out the pattern he had known as a child, but it crippled my heart with rejection, to be on the receiving end of similar treatment. I learned that dad's do not embrace their children easily.

I received one embrace as a little girl, which was extremely unwarranted and scarred me deeply for a long time. A family that stayed near to our house had a son who was a good bit older than me and unusually tall and strong for his age. His parents had a wooden shed in their back garden. One day he invited me to 'join his club'. I didn't know what that meant but I was attracted to the unique excitement of belonging. The exact details of the molestation are hidden in the mist of my small child's mind, but the memories of his hands and mouth invading places that stole my innocence along with the pain of that intrusion remained. I stored the trauma of that incident in the furthest recesses of my heart. I didn't tell. It was too grotesque to face the fear and shame that splintered my being.

### Mum made us laugh

Things weren't all bad. My mum had a good sense of humour and she always managed to make us laugh even during the bad times. She hugged us twice as much to make up for dad not being able to. When mum had too many bruises on her face to go out in public, she would keep us home from school. Those were special days, a secret from dad and others when we munched delicious trifles and watched stolen moments of TV.

Once my mum started a food fight during lunch! We children were eating tinned spaghetti and one of us was complaining. Mum picked up her fork, lifted a good helping of spaghetti and then flicked it across the table at the whinging sibling. Complete madness ensued with bits of spaghetti and toasted bread flying everywhere. At the end of our food fight we were covered in dollops of pasta and holding on to our stomach's, which were sore from laughing so hard.

Mum loved animals and we had all kinds of pets at one time or another. We had dogs, cats, budgies and fish. A stray cat once turned up at our door and gave birth to the tiniest kittens ever. They died one by one. We had tried to feed the last one with a doll's bottle filled with warm milk, but it was just too weak to feed. Mum kept it warm in her hand but after a valiant attempt it gave a single loud mew and died in her hands. We buried it in the garden and treated the shoebox coffin with sombre reverence. Goldfish that didn't make it were treated far less reverently. They were flushed down the toilet!

We adopted the stray cat and called her Cindy. She gave birth to a healthy litter of kittens a while later. They were the craziest kittens ever. They would make death-defying jumps and disappear into one fluffy ball of fur as they played at kitten wrestling. They made their home in a plastic Action Man tank of my brother's until it was time for them to find homes of their own (which was quite welcome really because we were getting a bit ticked off with the fleas they had been born with!).

We went on holiday as a family once a year. The highlight of going away was the time we spent at the beach. My dad was an ace sandcastle builder. We would search for seashells and decorate his golden coloured masterpieces with them. He would build castles and boats and we would never tire of running to the water's edge to fill our brightly coloured plastic buckets with sea water for the moat. We actually got to play with our dad and we revelled in it. The children had great fun burying dad in the sand and then seeing his big toes pushing through. We kicked a football around and sheltered from the wind behind a brightly coloured canvas windbreak. Trips to the beach were the only times we ever had picnics and the soggy warm tomato and ham sandwiches tasted all the more divine for their extra seasoning of gritty sand.

Sometimes I felt sorry for my dad. He told me he had grown up in a rough part of Glasgow, where gangs ran riot. His family had been poor and his mum died when he was only twelve, while he was in hospital recovering from his second bout of rheumatic fever. My grandpa used to beat my gran too.

### Names and pains that really hurt

At school I frequently got into scraps when people called my dad names. I was a fiercely loyal child. I hated what my dad did when he was drunk, but I still loved him. The kids at school were only telling the truth, but the truth hurt and I responded in the way my father had taught me – with my fists.

Not that I was much of a boxer! I was usually the one on the receiving end of being bullied at school. I was the smallest girl in a class of approximately twenty-five children and an easy target! I was regularly kicked, punched and ridiculed by boys and girls. I was a plucky child and fought back but I struggled daily to overcome fear.

When I was about nine or ten, a boy in my class gave me an unexpected gift. It was a box of peppermint creams. I thanked him for the sweets, but when I said 'no' to an invitation to date him, he responded by beating me up and left me sitting rumpled and bruised with a now somewhat bashed box of sweets - the peppermints were truly creamed!

Another peer issue that kept me on the outside looking in was that of my choice of music. I was a Donny Osmond fan whilst the other seven girls in my class were avid supporters of a boy band called Bay City Rollers. The Osmonds' were squeaky-clean cut and American. The Bay City Rollers were a tartan-clad army that every self-respecting Scottish teenager thought were brilliant – everyone, it seemed, except me. It was beyond my classmates understanding and they probably thought if they beat me often enough on this issue that I would change my mind. As opposition has a way of strengthening one's resolve on a matter, the thumps, likewise, just made my heart throb all the more for my teen idol Donny!

Desperate times call for desperate measures and I needed a strategy to stay out of trouble. I discovered that if I smiled a lot and fooled around I could generally get people to laugh. Having made them laugh, most of them would then forget to hit you! So in my search for survival techniques, the persona of Catherine the clown was born.

I made my mum laugh a lot too. When we were waiting for dad to come home from a drinking binge, I would dress up and sing silly songs in an attempt to make waiting for the inevitable less agonising. I did impressions and told the most awful jokes but I think mum appreciated my amateur efforts. When dad's car headlights appeared in the window, I would run up stairs at lightning speed and jump into my bed and feign sleep with my heart thundering in my chest. It wouldn't be long before the sickening thud of my mum being battered would drown out my heartbeat

### Witch persona?

There was another side to my personality, and in truth, it was quite weird. I knew things about people that I had no way of knowing. I didn't ever ask for it and I didn't know how to make it go away. I just knew about people and places and events before they happened. When I got older I found a name that seemed to suit my strange behaviour. I was somewhat psychic.

I discovered I had an ability to move objects if I concentrated on them. I remember visiting my gran when I was about four or five years old, and whilst sitting on the lounge floor I floated a copper penny out of a wooden bowl and behind the sofa. I was scared and excited all at the same time!

Then there were the metal objects. I could bend them! To my mother's chagrin, I re-shaped some of the contents of her cutlery canteen over the years. I went to a lot of trouble not to draw attention to myself, and only the odd spoon or fork would suffer a mind-bending remould. Without much effort I could usually tell who the authors of letters were before they were opened, as well as being able to identify a caller to our family home before the door bell rang or the telephone was answered. These bizarre incidents were normal to me along with all the other things that little girls do, daydreaming of being a princess chasing butterflies, and skipping, whenever I felt happy enough to do so.

I 'saw' things too, and I did not like that one bit! If I ever visited old buildings I would see ghosts. It would always get extremely cold just before they appeared. I suffered from the most appalling nightmares. The spiritual beings in my dreams terrified me much more than the bullies at school ever did. In short, I lived in two worlds. The physical one that every one could touch, and the 'other side' that I thought no one else could see but me.

## Meeting Jesus

It might surprise you to learn that despite all of the adverse things in my life, I attended Sunday school each week and enjoyed it immensely. I had a fascination for all things spiritual, and Jesus genuinely interested me. I watched Easter movies once a year and cried at the Man on the Cross. He was so beautiful. His gentle power drew me. It wasn't an overnight thing. He gradually won my heart.

At fifteen I went along to a School outreach and found myself captivated by the message of the Cross. I was too shy to go forward when the speaker made an appeal for people to come to the front. However, I approached some counsellors at the end of the meeting and dedicated my life to Christ. The team prayed for me and it felt like an electric current of powerflowing through my body. It was like nothing I had ever experienced before. It was around ten years later before I knew I had met the Holy Spirit!

I returned home on the coach and could hardly wait to tell my mum what had happened. I rushed in the door and proudly announced I had become a Christian. I was unprepared for what happened next. My mum was furious with me. She shouted at me and told me I was not a Christian. I was confused. We had been brought up to believe in God and now my mum seemed to be rejecting the very message she had encouraged us to embrace. I tried again and quietly said, 'Mum, I am a Christian, I gave my life to Jesus tonight'. Mum screamed at me this time and said again I was not. Now, with silent tears running down my cheeks, for the third time I whispered, 'Mum, I am a Christian, I've asked Jesus to be my Lord.' There were no more words, only a stinging slap as mum's hand hit my face – hard. This was my first experience as a Christian convert. My normally loving mother rejected my faith and persecuted me for being a believer.

**First love**

I didn't know any other Christians except for the teachers who led our small C.U. school group. It was there that I met a lovely boy called Stephen. He was a year older than me, tall and lanky with jet-black shiny hair. I now had two men in my life who made my heart flutter – Jesus and Stephen. Stephen was a believer too, and we talked a lot about the Bible and God stuff.

I encountered the power of the Holy Spirit during intense prayer times. For the first few months after my salvation, I wept night after night on the floor of my bedroom. With a dog-eared paper back bible I prayed God's word back to Him and asked him to save my dad and my whole family. I didn't know what the word intercession meant but I knew how to weep it with Jesus.

The bad dreams didn't go away, in fact, they got worse. My sleep was continually interrupted by foul nightmares and demonic intrusions into my bedroom. Things would fly around my room, my lamp would go on and off by itself, objects would be suspended in mid air. I was terrified and didn't know to whom I could turn.. I was so fearful of the condequences of telling.

# CHAPTER 2

## THE ROAD OF REBELLION

By the time I was seventeen my love affair with Jesus had cooled considerably. I just got distracted. I left school after passing my Higher-grade exams, hopeful to commence training in nursing. Leaving school also meant leaving behind the only source of Christian input I had. The romance with Stephen had fizzled out and he was long gone and my life as a believer slipped into words without actions.

Times turned turbulent at home. Mum and dad were legally separated, and I put aside my hopes of going to college. I chose to stay and support my mum and my younger brother. My sister was ill and was sent to recover at my grandparents. Dad attempted to commit suicide during this period and it felt as though the bottom had dropped out of my world. I was so angry. I was angry at God, angry with mum, angry with myself and really angry with my dad! I didn't know how to deal with all the rage I had, so I caged it deep inside and hit the road of rebellion; running hard with an aching, empty, heart.

The emptiness in my life began to be filled by occult deception. Sadly, I got drawn deeper into the realm of spiritual fantasy. I developed a compulsive dependency on horoscopes and star signs, becoming a prisoner to daily predictions as I scheduled my life around meaningless graphs and astrology. My mum sometimes took my sister and I to have tarot card and teacup readings. Over the years we visited caravans that housed spooky old ladies with crystal balls and met clairvoyants who spoke with eerie accents. Occasionally we attended psychic meetings where we were joined by other weary looking fortune seekers and broken hearted souls who wanted to know if their loved ones had passed safely over to 'the other side'! We were caught in a web of deception and in great need of divine intervention.

I started dating a guy who rode a motorbike. At that time dad used to hang around outside our new house and just wait in the moonlight, probably hoping for a glimpse of mum or one of the family. I deliberately ignored him. I knew he would be worried about me riding on a motorbike late at night, but I didn't care what he thought any more. I wanted him to hurt as much as I was hurting. We had a love-hate relationship that was boiling over into my militant mutiny from the dysfunctional family. Mum and dad were eventually reunited, but the 'normal' life soon resumed. I searched for a place to hide. . .

**Sex, drugs and rock & roll**

I met a different guy. He didn't drive a motorbike but he did play guitar and had long hair. He smoked dope and one night he let me try some. I liked the anaesthetic effect it had on my frazzled brain. I learned some rock songs and sang as a vocalist with his band and soon was able to 'toke the smoke' and head bang to metal music with the best of them.

I changed my image completely and wore customised jeans, denim jacket and leather cut off. I was proud of my hand painted t-shirts with pictures from my new favourite album 'Whitesnake'. I liked looking tough. It made me feel less vulnerable. I grew my hair and had it permed. I got engaged to the longhaired guitar player when I was seventeen. Two nights before this, he was arrested for receiving stolen goods. I started to smoke cigarettes that weekend and made my first trip to jail to visit my boyfriend.

I responded to the recurring violence at home by running away into an early marriage a few months before my eighteenth birthday. This life change caused me to spiral from one wrong decision to another. The occasional reefer became an expensive habit. I was addicted not only to hash and amphetamines but also to alcohol and was smoking around forty cigarettes a day. The next two years are mostly a blur of rock concerts and wild parties.

The clowning continued. I clocked up an amazing catalogue of mini disasters, which included breaking a toilet cistern and also flooding an entire kitchen because I thought I knew how to remedy a blocked pipe. The remedy I employed was simply to pull the pipe off the wall, which resulted in copious water damage and an emergency call to police and a plumber. I blew up several objects including a chicken, which exploded into a million pieces after the gas flame and glass dish it was resting in collided catastrophically.

I knocked myself unconscious on numerous occasions and on various obstacles including an attic opening and a desk drawer. I got stuck in the revolving glass revolving doors of a posh hotel, fell down several flights of stairs, broke an entire set of dishes in one sitting and these are just a few of the many incidents I could mention. Despite the hilarity my clumsiness often caused, inside I was still desperately unhappy. My first marriage was as stormy as my parents had been, and it ended after two years when my husband left me for another woman. In fairness to him, my conduct had been far from angelic.

In spite of the addictions, constant late nights and poor diet, I worked hard. By day I was a 'respectable' secretary and by night a bar maid, pulling pints and having my bottom pinched more times than I care to recount. One customer drove me to the end of my patience with his lewd actions and, after one remark too many I, later, poured an entire pint of beer over his head as he stood at the bar! Thankfully I didn't lose my job.

When I wasn't working I let my hair down and partied like there was no tomorrow and when tomorrow came I took painkillers by the handful to ease the throb in my head from being continually hung over. Strangely enough, I met Stephen one night in the midst of all the chaos. It was surreal to see him and talk again. He was gentle. It reminded me for a short time of my other First Love, but then I let it go. It was too painful to think. He disappeared as quickly as he had come.

### Young, single and not so free

After the marriage ended I stopped using drugs because I was too afraid to visit a dealer on my own! Over a period of time, depression had begun to plague me daily. The abandonment, by my first husband, for a woman twice my age, took its toll on my already chronically low self-image. I was, also, extremely paranoid because of the substance abuse. If you said 'boo' to me I jumped three feet in the air (well, almost). Everything was exaggerated. I loathed what I had become but felt helpless to change.

Although I was no longer smoking cannabis, I was still addicted to finding love. Carrying all the baggage of un-confessed sin, I staggered into the next few years of my life, self-destructing in a whirlwind of promiscuity as I desperately searched for love and affirmation in all of the wrong places. It seemed that no matter what, or how much, I gave of myself it was never enough to secure a stable relationship.

I swapped my dirty denims for sexy stilettos and exchanged the rock scene for the world of clubbing and 'Saturday Night Fever.' I morphed into a disco diva of the Eighties with big shoulder pads, even bigger hair, and clothes that bordered on the theatrically ridiculous with their glitzy appearance. It was the era of the New Romantics and I loved it! Alcohol took on a sophisticated new look with designer cocktails sporting natty paper umbrellas and the inevitable maraschino cherry. I drowned my sorrows and pretended I was in the paradise that the paper umbrella's alluded to. During this period, I became involved with a man who was a good bit older than I was. He was yet another guitar player whom I had met briefly at a party several years previously. He turned up at my door at 11:40 p.m. one evening and I stupidly let him in. I was so lonely and desperate for human company. It was to be a mistake of massive proportions. He was involved in dodgy activities of many kinds, including a fascination with spiritual 'travel'. He eventually stole my furniture and sold it after I had asked him to help me store it. Worse still, he raped me.

We had broken up as boyfriend/girlfriend a few months before and I met him unexpectedly at a party. It wasn't long before we were daring each other to race to reach the worm at the bottom of a bottle of Tequila. It ended in tears and trauma – mine. He forced himself on me and pinned me down with his hand over my mouth to stifle my screams. I sobbed silently and once it was over I managed to get a taxi home. Staggering into the sanctuary of my own house, I ran a scalding hot bath and began to scrub my skin till it was red and raw. However, no amount of scrubbing could remove the filthiness I felt at being raped. I was so ashamed because I had been drinking when it happened and partly blamed myself. It was years before I told anyone. I wondered if I was just getting what I deserved from the lifestyle I was living. Years later I understood that he was the type of man that preys on vulnerable women, which was my situation at that time. I was a victim– a victim of vicious circumstances.

With childhood violation still haunting the deepest recesses of my soul, I hit an all time low, feeling broken and utterly used and abused and my anger dissolved into a pit of despair. I was weary beyond words. The mask was cracking and acting the clown became impossible. I suffered a nervous breakdown and it was almost nine months later before I could resume normal activities (such as shopping), without bursting into tears or suffering from paranoid delusions. I moved back in with my parents, who helped me back on the road to health. My dad had calmed down a good deal since he had suffered a heart attack and he rarely took any alcohol. However, although I had returned home, my heart was still empty with loss. I was twenty-one years of age and believed the devil's lie that I was too much of a sinner to return to God.

### South Africa and back

I met and fell in love again. This time with an Englishman who had spent a lot of his life in South Africa (and yes, you've guessed it, he was a guitar player!) This romance took me on a sixteen thousand mile round trip in search of new beginnings. The month long trial I made to Johannesburg before considering a more permanent move was disastrous. I was ill with a serious kidney infection and lost more than a stone in weight. My boyfriend turned rat and spat vile accusations at me on the few occasions we did meet together. Most of the time, he just ignored me. Luckily, I smiled a lot and people were kind to me. My heart was broken yet again and I decided not to accept the job offers I had secured, but to return home to Scotland.

I spent my final night in Jo'burg doing a favour for a homosexual friend who worked for a famous make up company. They were launching a new range of products and planned to use a local swimming pool to create floating 'live' displays. A model dropped out at the last minute and I somehow managed to get volunteered. My role - to be an extra head dressed with Velcro rollers and pose on a float in the pool! Standing almost a foot shorter than most of the six foot leggy lovelies, with my face painted silver, my hair in fat rollers and wearing a metallic cape, I was utterly humiliated and felt as miserable as I looked. To add insult to injury my pasty white skin (which had turned a lovely colour of golden brown after much coxing) began to peel and great shreds of skin hung from my back in tatters. I felt like a total idiot and my future looked like my back – tattered.

The flight home was eventful, taking a full twenty-four hours rather than ten, because someone on board got extremely drunk and tried to assault a member of the cabin crew. The ensuing struggle involved three-cabin crew and a rope at the end of which, the drunken man found himself tethered to a seat at the rear of the plane! We were forced to return to Nairobi where the now dazed and sobered man was arrested and taken off the plane. We were then flown to Rome where a new flight crew were assigned to us, finally arriving in Glasgow much later than originally expected. I had been assigned a seat beside three Egyptian men whom I dubbed 'the three wise men'. They befriended me and joined heartily in an impromptu sing song (several vodkas later). Anything to dull the pain! They invited me to join them on their tour of Europe, promising I would have a room of my own. I was not at all convinced they did not have an ulterior motive, so I politely declined.

Back home reality hit hard and I kept myself to myself. The party animal retired. I didn't go out socialising at all. I was now a self-made recluse. The shoulder pads and stilettos went into early retirement and I moped about with no make up and greasy hair.

### Driving up the wall

I stayed home for almost a year, choosing instead to watch television and eat chocolate comfort food at night with mum and dad. My mum suffered her first heart attack and that was frightening. Dad especially was devastated at the thought of losing her, and it pulled us all closer together as a family. On the day mum was discharged from hospital, I decided to help out with the household chores. We had no food at home and I wanted to make a celebration dinner as a special surprise for her homecoming. At that time I had a provisional driving licence but was not authorised to be on the road without an experienced driver with me. Dad left to pick mum up, and for some inexplicable reason I decided to drive to the shops. I had no insurance, no parental permission and little by way of driving know-how! However, I managed to reach the local supermarket without incident, save for the copious amount of sweat I lost in nervous energy. Returning home I was extremely pleased with my purchases and myself.

Disaster struck as I attempted to negotiate the driveway at our house. I misjudged the opening and panicked, hitting the accelerator pedal instead of the brake pedal and smashed the front of the Sierra into the cement post. To my horror the car crunched up like a discarded sweet wrapper. I drove it to the end of the drive, and with head hung in shame I started operation clean up. By the time my parents arrived back there was no sign of glass or debris, the car was tucked away neatly (crumpled front well hidden) and the surprise meal was filling the kitchen with a delicious aroma. I was dreading breaking the news. Mum looked tired and fragile. I couldn't have felt more remorseful if I tried. Eventually I plucked up the courage to blurt out my misdemeanour. Dad was absolutely furious and took it personally, feeling that I had betrayed him. I cried and cried. I was so sorry. By way of restitution, dad insisted that I paid for half of the repairs. The total repair bill was almost £2,000. Ouch!

### New career

Escalating car costs necessitated an increased income! I opted for a career change and was fortunate enough to find employment with a training/recruitment agency. I truly enjoyed working with all kinds of different people. The job involved marketing to prospective employers with a view to securing job-training placements for Government trainees. These trainees were long term unemployed people whose names were registered on a data bank held by my employer. We matched trainees to work placements and hoped for a fruitful outcome for both.

I spent a considerable amount of time with the trainees themselves, getting to know them, doing regular reviews, visiting them in placement, conducting literacy and numeracy workshops etc. I found my new role both rewarding and challenging and started studying for a training qualification. Eventually I left the job on a point of principle, but it had given me invaluable experience and revealed I had good people skills.

**Here comes the bride - again!**

After almost a year of living like a hermit, I started dating again. I fixed my hair, put on my make up, and tried to hold my head up high. It was a whirlwind romance of only a few months and at the age of twenty-four, I married for the second time, with not a guitar player in sight! I became pregnant during the first month and was sick for the next nine! Mark was born in June 1989 and was worth every uncomfortable moment. After I readjusted to the lack of sleep, I took to mother hood like a duck to water. No one can prepare you for being a parent. No matter how many books you read on the subject, or people you take counsel from, the shock, of going without sleep on a regular basis, with a body that feels like it belongs to someone else, whilst your hormones are in orbit somewhere between planet earth and planet who-knows-where, is quite disconcerting. Mark was a great baby but vomited as much as his mother did during pregnancy.

**Back to work**

When Mark was just a few months old, I was approached by a different training agency and offered an excellent job prospect as a training consultant with a large retail chain. The post was part time and the money attractive. I decided to take the job and returned to a half working week. Mark was well looked after by my mother in law. I missed him during the times when I was gone from home, but he seemed to adjust well to the semi absence of mum.

I had a great time working as a training consultant. It was my first experience of public speaking and I learned quickly. My captive audience consisted of an energetic bunch of 16-18 year old retail trainees. I was twenty-five and the age difference between us was just sufficient to ensure a challenging but fun work environment. It was my responsibility to plan, prepare and deliver a programme of off-job training to my group of trainees. This covered a diverse range of subjects, which included topics such as retail law, kitchen planning, horticulture, communication, community project and even outward-bound team bonding exercises! I also made visits to nine different stores and attended store manager's meetings.

I studied hard and learned basic product knowledge; I picked the brains of the best department heads I could find and persuaded them to speak on subjects that were just too technical for me! I once got permission from the local courthouse to bring along a party of trainees for an in-house visit to let them experience the law environment first hand. The only difficulty was that the Judge sat for almost two hours, hearing one case after another without interruption. In desperation I stood up with a crimson face and said, 'Excuse me your honour, we need to leave now.'

The judge's gavel slammed the wood and he shouted angrily at me about contempt of court. I was horrified but didn't know how else to get his attention. A kind court official came to my aid and explained to the judge who we were and why we needed to leave. After a few agonisingly embarrassing moments we were finally permitted to leave without further complications. The trainees teased me for months about the 'excuse me' line.

On another occasion we were working on a community based project. The trainees had to think up a worthwhile project, as well as be responsible to fund and resource it. After raising money by carol singing they decided to perform a Christmas puppet extravaganza for the sick children at York hill hospital in Glasgow, many of whom were very seriously ill. Eventually the stage was built and the hand made puppets sewn together. After much heated debate, the team building had progressed from actual punch-ups to a much more demure level of screaming. The script was finally written and the day arrived to visit York hill.

There was a problem of gigantic proportions - we had become so engrossed in constructing the puppet theatre that we forgotten that it would have to be transported from the store to the hospital. In a panic we stuck the six foot wooden struts on top of my car and tied them with ropes. We piled into my tiny vehicle and hit the Glasgow motor-way. The red velvet stage curtains billowed from the car obscuring our vision and most of the oncoming traffic! It wasn't long before blue police sirens halted our progress. We stuttered out our 'predicament' to the 'boys in blue', and they were outrageously gracious to us and, instead of arresting us for dangerous driving, they gave us a police escort all the way to York hill Hospital! The children loved the puppet show and we were all deeply affected by their courage. We cried as we left, each one of us a little more humble than when we had first begun. The creative tantrums had been worth every moment to produce the smiles and genuine laughter in the children's hospital wing.

I regularly visited each of my trainees in their work place and was an agony aunt to them as well as a training officer. They confided in me and trusted me. I championed their cases when they were too intimidated to speak up for themselves to those in positions of leadership. I hated injustice and was a sucker for a good cause. My dedication and loyalty to my young 'trainees' sometimes got me into trouble with the store managers, but I think most people appreciated my sincerity. It gave me a buzz to see the trainees grow up and graduate. I delighted in their achievements and became more mature myself in the process. My contract ended abruptly due to a sudden change in government legislation. I returned to being a housewife and full time mum.

### Ugly intimidation

Sadly, the old monster of intimidation reared its ugly head again. During the four years of my second marriage I endured physical, mental and emotional torture. I was beaten, mocked, controlled and belittled on a regular basis. We had a lovely home, a nice car and my husband made good money working offshore, but I felt personally bankrupt. Things deteriorated to the point where I had no access to money and had to ask for handouts from my husband. I had hardly any friends and was afraid to talk to any one because my husband was obsessively jealous. The bullying of my early years at school paled into insignificance compared to my new lifestyle.

I became pregnant a second time but miscarried, losing the child at thirteen weeks. I was broken hearted and suffered from another black bout of depression. At home things were becoming increasingly unbearable and I reached the point of no return. The only reason I stayed was because I was afraid to go. I was in fear for my physical safety and made the decision to leave. I told my husband how I felt. He mocked me and thought I was joking. I made plans to leave him whilst he was working offshore. It may seem a cowardly thing to do, but I knew he would not have let me go if he was home. I just walked quietly out of his life with my little boy, then almost three years old.

I was a single parent, lonely, tired and broke. We moved into rented accommodation and struggled to get by. Financially, things were on hold while the lawyers sorted out child maintenance so I resorted to selling off the few scraps of furniture I had to my name to get money for food. Later, I received state benefit, and then child maintenance payments were credited, also. I was in need and made the wrong choice not do disclose my payments to the authorities. Eventually, all was revealed, and I had to repay all the state money I had received. I was glad because I had felt so guilty about stealing, but tried to justify it, at the time, because I couldn't pay my bills.

### The return of Stephen

One shiny ray of hope for the future appeared on my misery filled horizon – Stephen came back into my life. The very same lanky sixteen year old I had known at school suddenly came back to Scotland! He called me on the telephone one evening and we struck up a friendship again. It was a relief to have him around. He genuinely seemed to care and he didn't threaten me and liked Mark a lot.

I relocated to a small village and after initially receiving hate mail and having to put up with bricks being thrown at my door, things began to settle down. The divorce was long and drawn out, with each point being contested. Meanwhile, my friendship with Stephen blossomed into romance. The only way I knew to give love was through physical affection and within a few months I conceived again. The news rocked our world. We moved in together and awaited the arrival of our child.

# CHAPTER 3

## GETTING TO KNOW DAD

My relationship with my dad had changed a lot during the three years after Mark was born. As a papa he was a pussycat! He showered my wee boy with love and affection and it was a healing salve to my heart to watch them together. Mark followed his papa everywhere whenever he had the chance to do so. Mark still spent time with his dad and other relatives, but he had a special place in his heart for my father. The hardness of heart from times gone by seemed to melt away from dad as he spent time with his grandson. He stopped drinking several years previously and this enabled each of our family members to begin to trust again.

My dad and I were becoming much closer. I had begun to forgive him in my heart for the ways in which I had been robbed of his love as a child. I saw another side to him, a far more gentle and loving side. My opinion of him was changing. We talked, we listened to each other, and we laughed together. I was finding my dad, and it felt so good. One day as we were walking up the garden path, my dad took hold of my hand and held it for the first time in as long as I could remember. It was a beautiful clear day and the sun was shining down on us. My heart melted as he looked at me and even though his lips couldn't express the love he felt, it was one of the most precious moments we ever had together.

When I found out I was pregnant I experienced a stirring to go to church. It was as though I had a magnet in my body that was being drawn to metal. I was really happy to be carrying this new child inside me, but I felt the need to make peace with the Gentle One who seemed to be calling me again to turn from being a prodigal and come back home. I was so nervous at the thought of entering a church building after so many years of absenteeism on my part that it took me several weeks of walking by the front doors before I finally had the nerve to go in.

I shuffled anonymously to the upstairs gallery. Red-hot shame was burning my face a blistering red colour, but I stayed nonetheless. It was quiet up stairs. I don't remember the preacher's message, only the wave of forgiveness that poured down on me. I thought of my years in the world and of all the awful things I had done during that time. I realised how undeserving I was of this magnificent Love falling all over me. I didnot say a word, I didn't know how, and I didn't have to because Jesus was looking deep inside my heart. I simply opened up to the only One who could bring Peace and healing to my aching heart. In the silence I returned to my Saviour. I walked out the church into a new beginning. God had given me a secondchance. Just a few days later, on the evening of September 25th, 1993, without warning, my father dropped dead. I was stunned.

The shock of his sudden passing was a body blow of massive proportion. I rocked back and forth on my bed, my pillow soaked with sorrow-filled tears from swollen eyelids. My head was full of memories, good and bad, and it felt as though my heart would explode with the loss.

On the third day of mourning my father, I cried out to God, 'I have no daddy' and in that heart rending moment the Lord spoke to me with exquisite tenderness, 'Precious child, I Am your Father.' For the first time I heard my heavenly Father's voice and understood in the depth of my being that he was my Dad as well as my Saviour. I curled up and imagined I was sitting in his lap. It was just like being small all over again and my wounded soul listened in wonder as I heard the sweet lullaby of my Father's song of love for me. It turned my world inside out and ushered in a deep work of God in my life. He, who desires truth in the inner soul, came to heal and put in place a new foundation.

### The Father's heartbeat – a vision
*"We love because he first loved us"* 1 John 4:19

I soon began to experience the Holy Spirit in some beautiful ways. One day I sensed Jesus begin work on my ears. He removed a small black object from my inner ear. I asked Jesus what this was and he replied, "These are lies that have been spoken into your life." He then removed the object, which released healing from the effects of these lies and this enabled me to hear him with greater clarity.

The Lord then attached a small earphone to my ear. It looked fairly high-tech! I was impressed! He plugged the end of the lead of the earphone into his chest. I laughed out loud because I could hear his heart beat! The Lord laughed too, most probably, at my child-like giggles. It was delightful to hear his heartbeat so clearly. The Lord then instructed me to open my mouth. As I carefully responded to his instructions, I began to speak and a glorious Light emanated from my mouth. The more intently I listened to his heartbeat, the greater the intensity of Truth that came out of my mouth.

The vision changed and I saw a little girl playing hide and seek with her father. She had her eyes closed, but was listening intently for his footsteps. He came to his daughter, sat down with her then lifted her onto his knee. She immediately yielded to his tender embrace and cuddled into him. She looked earnestly into his face, keen to hear her father's words. He said, "Sweetheart, you don't have to play hide and seek to find me - I will come when you call".

I was struck by the simple picture of a small child in her father's arms and of the powerful reality that similarly, God our Father really does want us to spend time with him. It's not a game although it is delightful and it isn't a burden for Father to respond to his children. He loves it when we call his name! He longs for us to draw near and receive his embrace.

The little girl smiled at her father and he gazed lovingly at her. She rested her head on his chest and I was able to hear the same heartbeat I had a moment before. I felt her peace and the tenderness and depth of Father's love washed over me in a new measure. I received deeper understanding of God's awesome and absolute care and protection of his children.

Peace saturated my being.

The beat of the Father's heart still echoes in my ear.

# PART II

# THE DEEP

*Deep .adj. 1 extending far down or in from the top or surface
2. very intense, profound, or extreme.
Difficult to understand*

# CHAPTER 4

## A JESUS FREAK?

The day of my father's funeral arrived uninvited and darkly melancholic. The sky was grey and showered us in deep, drenching rain that the black undertaker's umbrellas could not quite protect us from. In contrast, a beautiful medley of bright flowers adorned the coffin. A white and yellow cross along with a flower arrangement that spelt the word 'DAD' had pride of place amongst the many others in the shiny black hearse. It was difficult to believe we were burying my father. My heart was breaking as we listened to the haunting Celtic lilt of the tune 'Danny boy' being played on a small tape recorder at the graveside as my father's coffin was slowly lowered into the ground. The wet earth hit the casket with a deafening thud as the minister prayed out, 'ashes to ashes, dust to dust' and just like that, my dad was gone. Death had made my father larger than life.

For some time I agonised over the question of dad's eternal residence. I had never heard him confess to being a believer in Jesus, yet he had a deep reverence for God. In my grief, I recalled the intense prayer times I had on his behalf just after I was converted. I found a resting place for my anxious thoughts. Death had come and gone but it was time to move on and discover a new kind of 'normal' and my swelling abdomen helped to focus my attention on life.

The months that followed Dad's death found me in the doldrums despite the discovery of God as my heavenly father. There was no quick fix to my complex distortion of self-image but things were beginning to stir deep in my being. I felt waves of forgiveness each time I thought of my father and cried at what had been and what could never be. The questions that filled my head became a precursor to the next five years of healing. I thought everything was my fault but in the inner recesses of my mind I knew that couldn't be true. How could I be healed of the things that should never have been done to me? They had shaped my life as I sought a way to escape from the pain. Despite the injustice, I recognised the need to take responsibility for my own actions.

My heart was sincere but I seemed to constantly fail in the area of spiritual victory. I wanted to be obedient to God but whilst my spirit was willing, my flesh was extremely weak. I was spiritually immature and struggled with sin. I loved God and didn't mean to be rebellious but my lifestyle hardly mirrored the purity I longed to walk in. I was living with Stephen and was confronted by the paradox of grace – I saw how real my own sinful desires were, but despite my self-loathing, I was astonished by the revelation that I was still lovely to God. God met me in the midst of my spiritual crisis with his divine affection. He enabled me to run into his loving embrace and not away from it. My heart was captivated by his tenderness and it ignited the beginnings of my journey to victory in Grace.

Despite my sorrow at losing my father, I was quietly excited about the prospect of new life that lay ahead. On Christmas Eve of '93, Stephen proposed to me under the stars, and we were both keenly aware of the Father of Lights, and his hand on our future together. I was engaged to be married and yearned for legitimate love. It felt as though my own life was beginning to mirror the romance of the gospel! Stephen and I wanted to get married straight away, but the divorce continued to be long and drawn out. Quite unexpectedly, our baby decided to make a surprise arrival almost three weeks before the due date. Daniel burst into our lives on Mother's day, 13th March 1994. He was a beautiful child, dark haired and dark eyed. Mark was so excited to have a little brother to play with.

We settled into a reasonable routine in our small home that over-looked a wooded glen. I made friends with a Christian girl who never judged our domestic arrangements, but simply loved us through them. Stephen sometimes drank too much and that put a consider-able strain on our home life. Months passed uneventfully until, at last, the decree nissi arrived and we were able to set a date for our wedding. We chose February 14th 1995 – Valentine's Day!

### Love, lies and freedom

In the interim period, I wrestled with a lifetime worth of lies that the enemy had planted in my heart. My dad had broken promises but I held on to the truth that God was a covenant keeper; Jesus had been rejected so that I might be accepted. My dad hadn't listened to me when I was little, and I didn't talk much to him either, but despite this I pursued my relationship with God with fervency because I wanted the silence to end. I discovered I liked to talk! My dad hadn't held me but I believed that God my Father loved me without condition. The simplicity and mystery of the Gospel was my new plumb line for nor-mality.

In the midst of seeking my sanity in God, a strange manifestation of evil invaded our home. It began just after I had a realisation that the psychic gift I had operated in since childhood wasn't from God. The thought just hit me one day like a tonne of bricks caving in on an unsuspecting passer by. I had simply never considered the source of my 'second sight'. I just lived in it. God spoke to my heart and opened my spiritual eyes to the deception. Finding God as Father had created an access point from his heart to mine. It enabled him to speak to me about Truth and at that point in my life, I really did need some clear definition!

By way of retaliation, the devil did not go away. Instead, I was aware of a dark presence that followed me everywhere like a cloud. It hung around me and sulked. The sulking didn't last long and soon it was hurling abusive comments at me. The demon mocked me daily, stating that it would not go away and that I could not make it. The demon was right. I had no idea what to do about it. For several months, I put up with the terror it inflicted on my heart and mind. I told nobody. Fear had a way of making me catatonic.

Almost at my wits end, I finally realised that God wanted to set me free from the hold the demon had on my life. I decided to ask someone for help. I didn't know anything about the theology of demonic oppression or possession; all I knew was that there was a demon bothering me, that it would not go away and I wanted it gone!

I set out to find someone who would pray with me. I went to a Christian meeting and approached a friend who was also a mature believer and leader. I asked him to help me. He told me to command the demon to leave in the name of Jesus. I did. All I remember about the next forty minutes is that Jesus was nearer than my next breath. I hit the floor immediately and found breathing almost impossible. My face was congested and my eyes stood out on stalks. I could hear a horrible scraping voice emitting from my throat. I bounced around the floor of the hall for what seemed liked an age. The demon was not happy about his eviction. I heard people praying in strange tongues I didn't understand. I was soaked through with sweat and exhausted from being thrown around the room. Suddenly it was over. Everything was still and looked brand new. Things even sounded differently. I sat silently for a very long time, marvelling at Jesus my Saviour and Strong Deliverer. There were only a few people left in the room, which before had been crowded. Soft worship music soothed my soul.

The next day I received a phone call from a lady who had witnessed my deliverance experience. She explained that something similar had happened to her a long time ago and that I might feel tired and emotional. She was right. I felt exhausted. My face was covered in tiny pinprick bruises, and my throat was raw. My limbs hurt from their dramatic encounter with the floorboards and I was confused and wondered about what had happened the night before. I was embarrassed that so many others had been onlookers. The lady told me not to worry, and that I ought not let the devil rob me of my healing. I truly appreciated her kindness and encouragement. Little did I know then how well acquainted I would become with floors and carpets during ministry sessions!

### A Jesus freak?

Several days later, I received another phone call from a believer who had attended the meeting and was upset by what she had seen. She wanted me to know that she had called our minister to express her concerns. She told me she didn't think I had ever really been a Christian because I had had a demon living inside me. How could I answer her? I just told her I was sorry she had been upset and, that I did not understand it either. I had loved Jesus before the experience, and loved Him more now. I felt like a freak, but life went on. In ignorance, the church can sometimes be quite callous.

The demonic eviction left me with a sense of emptiness. Surely, there was more to Christian living than going to meetings every so often? How did God get to invade your space? I decided I wanted more of God but was not sure how to go about getting it. I committed to going to church more regularly. I had a Bible, but only read it occasionally. It accompanied me to church but it wasn't really a source of daily bread. It was several years before I realised that if I wanted God's wisdom I needed to read His word! I prayed sometimes, but much of it was experienced in my head i.e. silently. I was slightly bored and not fully committed to pursuing God whole-heartedly. My enthusiasm ebbed and flowed.

One evening, I attended a Supper Service at the local church. Although most people were friendly, I was still unsure of myself and felt extremely nervous. When someone instructed us to split into small groups to pray, I was so frightened that I ran right out the hall and once outside, burst into tears. I still smoked at the time, so I lit a cigarette and drawing deeply on the tobacco I said, 'God, I can't do this.' He spoke gently to my heart and said, 'yes, you can'. It was a major moment and I recorded it in my diary as the time when the mouse (me) met the Lion of the Tribe of Judah (Jesus). Amazingly, I found the strength to go back into the hall. I was shaking all over but I sat down and joined a group to pray. I muttered a few incoherent words but it was a significant breakthrough for me.

I joined a small house group that met during weeknights. It was an additional meeting place to Sunday mornings. The group consisted of women of different ages who met in each other's homes to study the Bible and pray. I was the youngest and the least experienced. The songs were screechy and the praying was a bit scary but I decided to hang out with them any way. I wanted to learn how to be a Christian and it felt like a good place to begin.

One night, an old lady came to the meeting who was sick. I longed to pray for her but I was not confident enough to do so. I watched while the other women went over, and placed their hands on her, and started to pray. They spoke in strange languages. I was desperate to join in but I couldn't pray like them. When I did manage to verbalise my prayers they usually came out in stilted English.

Despite myself, my trembling legs took me to her side and my sweaty palm somehow found its way to her back. I closed my eyes, and thought about Jesus, and, how He had healed me. Tears began to roll down my cheeks at my own impotence in prayer. Silently, I begged the Lord to help me. Instantly, I felt red-hot heat in my hand and simultaneously I opened my mouth and a new language gushed out in a torrent of God power. I had absolutely no idea what I was saying, but the compassion of God poured through me, causing me to shake uncontrollably. My tears of frustration turned to tears of joy. God met me in my inability to do anything, and the Holy Spirit prayed through me. The old lady was healed, and I could now speak in tongues!

# CHAPTER 5

## FACING THE BROKENNESS

In January 1995 we moved into a beautiful four bedroom house with panoramic views of the countryside. Our new home was spacious and we were thrilled and surprised to be there. I became preoccupied with wedding plans and preparations. We faced a moral dilemma – how could we honour God while we waited for our wedding day? We had two lovely sons, but were living as common law husband and wife. Stephen and I opted for a period of celibacy before the wedding, which lasted a couple of months. It seemed an appropriate thing to offer Jesus by way of denial. It was a gift from our heart to His. The wedding day arrived and sixteen years after meeting my first love at high school, I finally married Stephen. Our teenage love had spanned almost two decades to find fulfilment on our wedding day with Jesus at the centre.

Being married made a huge positive impact on my insecurity. The covenant I had made before God with Stephen unlocked an unspoken trust that enabled me to begin to face the breadth of my inner brokenness. I had spent much of my life in denial and now there was nowhere to run. It was necessary to face the captivity and bondage that abuse, sin and wrong choices had heaped on my life. The love of my Father and my husband was an anchor as the storm raged internally on the issue of my identity. The 'Who am I' of yesteryear returned to haunt me with malicious intent, but I pressed in to find my true identity and the depth of the heart of God. I wanted to be in the flow of what God was doing whether or not I was in the right place at the right time.

My Father was keen to help me understand that I had a birthright from which I had run. As I struggled to 'get my head round it' He showered me with hope and holy friendship.

### Badly expressed anger

I had been angry for so long I hardly noticed the feelings of deepseated rage, which I carried as excess emotional baggage. Receiving the deliverance healing moved me from energyless passivity into the realms of badly expressed anger! I believe God allowed me to experience these emotions in order to help me face the past. I could never know the fullness of what He promised for tomorrow unless I let him heal me from the savage pain of my yesterdays. Stephen and I met regularly with our minister, for counselling about my anger. The emotions I experienced were so hateful that I was afraid I might hurt myself, or someone else. I walked a fine line between self-control and totally losing it. We prayed into some issues and asked Jesus to restore my memories. I had only a few childhood recollections, most of which were awful. They were stored layer upon agonising layer in the attic of my mind, where their decaying weight threatened to engulf my soul. I was on an emotional roller coaster yo-yoing between anger, fear, depression and nothingness.

### Restoration of innocence

God intervened and rescued me in a melodramatic moment. His healing and release came in an unexpected way. My innocence had been stolen as a child and I was surprised by God's restorative remedy. In the middle of asking questions about my anger, God made Himself the answer to my seeking. I made a last minute decision to attend a series of seminars on emotional healing. At the end of the week of teaching I responded to an invitation to prayer. I remember closing my eyes and seeing a little girl. It was me! Jesus came and stood by my side and placed his hand on my shoulder. I heard a noise that made my blood run cold. It was the loudest, most painful scream I have ever listened to. I opened my eyes and was shocked to see that it was my mouth the scream was coming from. Other people in the room looked afraid.

I quickly closed my eyes again, and experienced another vision of Jesus. The screams subsided into body racking tears. It felt as though a waterfall was cascading over my head and back. I was convinced I was soaking wet. Peace began to saturate my being. In the vision, Jesus gave me a beautiful white dress to wear and placed a silk ribbon in my hair. I felt completely clean and fresh. My innocence had been restored. It was a miracle of healing in my heart. The scream had been necessary. I could not be content with what I was, until I was able to say, "how can that be?" The healing tears that Jesus had wept with me dissolved my anger.

### On the wings of a prayer...

On the wings of a prayer
You led me to completeness in you.
Head hung in despair you tilted my eyes
Until they were full of your glorious light.
As a scream rent through me,
The years of not knowing
The swiftness and severity were enough to almost kill me.
But you held me so tightly, never once letting go.

## The Normal, The Deep and The Crazy

In your mercy, you withheld the awful truth,
Until in your perfect timing, tiny trickles in my memory began to
flow
Into a seemingly unending river.

And rage, like a dam about to burst was full to overflowing.
And the fear was all encompassing, icing up your Fatherhood
The shame of stolen innocence burned hotly in my blood.
The mask was cracking and I was being torn apart,
But I knew you were holding my hand.
Your strength and tenderness pervaded every part of my being.
From the deepest place of despair I called to you
And you found me.

In those memories you poured in your love,
In rivulets and rainbows your nearness washed away the grubby
and Grimy vestige of the child who was weeping.
You spoke of little nonsense's as your Spirit ministered to me.
You gave me a beautiful new white dress to wear and a ribbon for
my hair.

As you wiped the tears from my face,
You gently lifted the shame and the guilt and fear from me.
You spoke, 'little one, these were never yours to carry.'
I recall how still the moment was.
I recall the intensity of your presence,
The myriad emotions in the sparkle of your eyes.
I remember living waters cascading over me without beginning or
end
And the freshness of being washed clean.

I remember the awesome sense of wonder
As I found you again as my Father.
That inexplicable joy, which had eluded me for so long was mine
now
(as it had always been), revealed for all eternity.

In the days that followed there was no more hollowness.
No more searching.
What had been stolen – you had returned.

## Facing The Brokenness

There may still be days when I will stand only by your Grace;
days when the enemy will return to try and rob me.
But in those days, I know that you have taken me far above all this
and in victory,
in Jesus name,
You fly with me
… on the wings of a prayer ….

# CHAPTER 6

## ONLY WHEN IT HURTS

Just a few weeks into our marriage, I discovered I was pregnant again! The timing was not quite what we had planned, but once we got over the initial shock we were all delighted. I had been taking contraceptive pills but in my usual dizzy manner had forgotten to swallow them at the same time each day. Apparently, this had an effect on their ability to prevent a pregnancy – it was true!

Being pregnant for a third time was much more of a strain that I had anticipated. I was physically exhausted. I became anaemic, and also developed pregnancy diabetes. My weight, along with the weight of my growing baby, rocketed as a direct result. The baby was in breech position for the duration of the pregnancy. I was uncomfortable and huge. The gynaecologist decided I should have a Caesarean section. I was not happy!

The scheduled date arrived, and I was admitted to hospital for an operation the following day. I was desperate for my baby to arrive in God's timing and I went to prayer. Within a few hours, my waters broke and in the middle of the night a hasty call was made for Stephen to come to hospital. Despite the plans for a scheduled c-section, the operation became an emergency one. Complications developed with the anaesthetic, and, unfortunately, it didn't work! In theatre, the first cut to my abdomen was made, and I was in absolute agony. I felt the surgeon's scalpel cutting into my stomach and tears ran down my face. The anaesthetist apologised and offered to render me unconscious immediately, but my baby was being delivered, in front of my eyes, and I wanted to see him or her. I opted for maximum epidural and morphine once the procedure revealed the identity of our little one.

It was a girl! Stephen and I cried tears of wonder filled joy. We had two beautiful sons and now a gorgeous wee girl made three. We called her Rebecca. She was a big baby for a small lady like me to deliver – 9 lbs and 8 oz. Rebecca's legs were in a strange position when she was born, due to the awkward breech. However, with careful monitoring, and prayer, the problem was resolved. A year later, she was given the all clear.

### Baby blues and belonging

It took me much longer than I had expected to get back on my feet, physically and emotionally. It was incredibly painful to walk after the operation. I was weak and cried much more than I had done with the other babies. Day three after delivering a baby is usually the time when most women cry a lot because of a hormone rush. I started to weep then and didn't feel much like stopping.

I came home and, unfortunately, my wound refused to heal properly. I developed an infection, which turned into a secondary infection, which turned even nastier when the third course of antibiotics proved ineffective. Thankfully, Rebecca was a wonderful child. She ate and slept effortlessly and was content from the moment she entered the world. Her gentle nature was evident from the beginning.

After a few weeks I was finally able to get up and about again but I just wasn't able to shake the baby blues. I tried to pray but God felt far away. I had come such a long way in overcoming massive emotional wounds in the past two years but it seemed there was still something adrift. Here with my family I should have felt complete, but instead I struggled anew with my sense of belonging. Holding my baby daughter brought me deep joy but it also caused me to look again at my own position as a daughter. God was firmly established in my life as Father, but was I as confident of my own position as his daughter? He was fully mine, but was I wholly His?

I reflected back to my own childhood and considered that I sometimes missed the numbness my soul used to feel. The love of God was wonderful but it hurt to continually be confronted with the past. Bit by bit God was putting my broken heart together but things got worse before they got better. The depression didn't go away. My mind was preoccupied with thoughts of the past and of the future, but the present just blurred into the obscurity of a robotic domestic routine.

My depression was clouding my rational ability to think and I was drowning in a sea of worthlessness. I truly did not want to inflict my pain on anyone else. I made covert plans to leave Stephen and the children because at the time I genuinely believed they would be better of without me. The devil hurled horrendous accusations at me. He screamed lies until shame covered my ears and I couldn't discern Truth anymore. I was lonely, afraid and convinced I did not deserve a husband and three beautiful children. I certainly did not think I was a good mother or wife. I didn't understand then as I do now, that one of the devil's techniques of torture is to remind us of our past lives and who we were, in order to prevent us from overcoming fear and moving into new realms of faith.

I was ready to leave. My getaway route was planned and the letters I would write explaining why I had left were imprinted on my heart. My credit card would be my initial means of support and I intended to borrow the car. I couldn't sleep. It was the dead of night and if I was going to leave, the time was now. I sat up in bed and looked at Stephen. He was sleeping peacefully and the devil tried one last time to convince me of my failure. Jesus happened in that moment. The Holy Spirit moved on me and I touched Stephen's shoulder. His sleepy eyes opened and he looked at me in love. I started to cry. It was a long time before I could speak. He held me until the tears flowed into words. I confessed my plans to him and asked him to help me. He was calm, but I think quite shocked. God was in the house and watching over us. We talked a lot after that. I realised that I was clinically depressed and that the hormones were playing a large part in that. I got some medication from the doctor, but the greatest medicine was the Hand of God on my life and the constancy of Stephen's love despite my erratic emotions.

I held on to my Saviour as tightly as I knew how, desperate to believe that God would not let me down. It was only a short time since I had spoken with Stephen about leaving. I still felt a bit shaky. I decided to go out alone in the car. The driving conditions were ideal; it was a crisp and clear night and sparkling stars lit the night sky. I thought everything was ok. I got into the car and drove off with no particular place to go.

In a short space of time the darkness of the sky resonated in my soul. The devil was trying to convince me to end my life. I was approaching a tree at high speed, but for once, everything within me fought back. I wanted to live. I wasn't going to succumb to suicide but the ensuing struggle for survival was intense nonetheless. I wrestled with an unseen force as it tried to take over the driving wheel. I shouted out loud and told Satan to back off, because I belonged to Jesus. I was His and He was mine and that was that. The car stayed on track and so did I. For the first time ever, I saw angels. Stars did not only light the night sky now, but also sweeping angelic beings. I was breathless in belonging to God, and supremely aware that he was truly watching over my every moment.

### A doll for a daughter

I wanted to buy Rebecca a doll but couldn't bring myself to do so. I decided to ask Jesus to help me understand the reason why not. He reminded me of one of my earliest memories, which was of my father bandaging my mother's ribs, several of which he had broken by punching her. Understandably I had been traumatised by what I saw. To try to make things up to us, my father had bought my sister and me a doll. I hated that doll with a passion and now, as an adult, I realised it had become the unwitting target on which I vented my pain and anger at my dad, initiating two decade's worth of doll loathing!

I couldn't do anything with the hurt in my heart at that point, but I was overwhelmed by a compelling urge to buy a doll for myself. At the age of thirty-one I set out to voluntarily purchase my own doll! During a family trip to Spain we located a market and Stephen took off with the children and left me to browse, unhurried, amongst the stalls. Eventually a particular doll caught my eye. She had brown curly hair and was dressed in a daisy print dress and wore the cutest smile you've ever seen. I bought her, took her home and named her Megan.

It was time to let go of the pain. I felt small and scared again but I sat down with my doll and asked God to forgive me for being so angry with my dad and to heal me from the awful memory that had been the trigger for such pain. I hugged my doll and wept unrestrainedly, allowing my heavenly Father to hold me and let His Love wash away my fear and anger at my earthly father. It was another huge milestone on my road to complete emotional recovery. I was learning to be a trusting daughter.

### Prophetic healing

The Lord continued to lead me into wholeness in Him; His intention was to heal me from every wound, which included even my earliest memories. He did this by introducing me to the beauty of prophetic healing through a South African woman. She was a wonderful teacher and I thoroughly enjoyed her message and down to earth manner. After preaching, she prayed and prophesied over the congregation. I was amazed at the way in which God used her to speak into the life situations of the people present. I had never seen or heard anything quite like it. I recognised the hallmark of Jesus in her words and humble prayers and was riveted as word after word of God speaking flowed from her.

After almost two hours of praying for people without stopping, the South African woman walked towards me and took my face in her hands. It was as though Jesus Himself held me and spoke to me through her. I do not remember much of what was prayed, but God ministered to the tiny baby I had been in my mother's womb. Through prophetic imagery, God revealed this had been the starting point of my life long struggle with fear and rejection. In addition to the prayers for healing, this wonderful lady also prayed for a release in the gift of prophecy in my life. It was to be a prayer of impact in my journey with Jesus, for it ignited a holy passion for God's Voice that could not be quenched!

God was determined to root out fear in my life. Over the next few months, the Holy Spirit highlighted different memories, which had been access points for satanically induced fear in my life. Horrific images of blood, broken furniture and bruises from childhood assaulted my soul; terror filled incidences of my rape, attempted suffocation, being urinated upon, being used as a human ash tray, brutal beatings and many other foul instances invaded my senses, but God healed me by bringing the Peace and the Presence of Christ into each one. God had been there and heard me when I cried. He was still listening and I was still crying but each new tear washed away the grime and grubbiness I felt from the past, bathing me in God's unconditional love. This was the only effective antidote to fear and my refuge from Satan's violation. Jesus was my alibi of Grace.

### A legitimate heir

My initial healing years were sealed by a sovereign move of God that brought me to a place of experiential understanding of my legitimacy as a child of His own. In studying the Scriptures, I was upset to discover that no Israelite born of a forbidden marriage, or any of their descendants could ever enter the assembly of the Lord, even down to the tenth generation. (*Deuteronomy 23:2*) I meditated on my own illegitimacy and that of my son. For several days, I prayed about it and in desperation asked God to help me.

The Holy Spirit was God's love messenger as He led me in a time of asking forgiveness. I surrendered to the process of repentance and as I did this, hidden anger at my mum and dad surfaced in my heart because I, too, had been conceived outside of marriage. I forgave them and asked Jesus to forgive them too. I broke the curse of illegitimacy in my family line and released a blessing on my children. It was finished. The girl who had run away from her God-given inheritance finally found her place in her father's kingdom. I was a child of God and an heir to all that Jesus had promised. As if to confirm this, I saw a spectacular rainbow as I gazed out the window. It spoke to me of God's faithfulness to keep his promise no matter what, and a new leaf turned in the pages of my life.

*'Because you are sons, God sent the Spirit of his Son into our hearts, the Spirit who calls out, 'Abba, Father.' So you are no longer a slave, but a son; and since you are a son, God has made you also an heir.'*

*Galatians 4:6, 7*

# CHAPTER 7

## THE BIRTH OF A WORSHIPPER

I accepted God's restoration in my life and He released me into new realms of discovering His Voice. This caused an immediate response in my heart and mind, which overflowed into what I did with my time and who I chose to spend time with. It was mostly Jesus! The bottom line was, I wanted to please God and was willing to do just about anything He asked me to do.

Each time I had been pregnant I gave up smoking, only to start again once each of my babies were born. It was frustrating to have stopped three times and then start again. Not long after Rebecca's birth, I was puffing away on a cigarette. I remember standing in my kitchen with a lit cigarette, talking to Jesus. Suddenly, his voice spoke a clear instruction, *'Catherine, put that cigarette out now.'* It was gentle, but insistent. I ran the cold-water tap, extinguished the cigarette in the running water and have never smoked since. In my own strength I couldn't give up but with God's help I was able to kick my nicotine 'habit' with relative ease.

I quickly discovered that being popular with God does not necessarily make you popular with people. I thought more and more about Him. I became intense as I pursued my faith and the people around me were intimidated. My long-term non-Christian friends were freaked out by the new me and backed off. Most of my Christian friends did the same. Their disapproval was mostly unspoken but I felt as though I was an embarrassment to them. I did not fully understand this response but I didn't let it hold me back. It seemed strange to me that when I had been spiritually impoverished and ignorant it appeared to bother anyone. Now, as an emerging young adult believer, I appeared to get on everyone's nerves!

Many of the first people to throw stones of accusation at me about being an 'over the top' Christian were those who knew God's call on their lives but, for whatever reason, were not fulfilling it. I learned to bounce back and it helped me to mature as a believer. My passion was a proverbial pain in the neck to those whose love for Christ had grown a bit cold, or whose hearts were distant from Father. I positively hated the religious façade that Christians wore.

I longed for demonstration not imagination of the gospel. God taught me to deal with disapproval and to love them regardless of whether or not I was accepted or rejected. It wasn't easy for me to do this and I cried a lot in the process, but as I learned to do this I grew in God. I wanted anointing not religion. God was moving the mountain of sin in my life and His Grace was so real to me. I rejected the insipid and passionless Jesus of so many. My God was a God of power and my passion for him was unadulterated and unashamed. I refused to let bitterness take root in my heart, and earnestly pursued God's call on my life.

I seemed to outgrow my Christian companions, without meaning to. I was unable to meet people on the terms they were determined to impose, and the political structure of church policy was difficult to embrace. I didn't sound, or look, like most of the people around me. Why could they not accept me as I was? Why did everyone want me to change to look like they looked? What was so wrong with a blazing heart shouting, 'God, send me?' Was the name calling and labelling of others really necessary? Why was it so important to conform to a certain spiritual image to which I could never relate?

Jesus said, *'go and make disciples of all nations'* – he didn't say they all had to look and sound the same. It is his image we are called to reproduce not our own. I didn't mean to be rebellious. I simply wanted a revolution for the kingdom, and I was certain being a Christian did not mean I had to become a compromised clone, or simply hang around and play word games.

I was zealous and lacked wisdom. At times the arrogance of youth kept me blind to this fact until I had matured a bit more. Looking back, I realise that whilst my love for Jesus was beautiful and commendable, being intense didn't mean I was mature. Yet, God was patient as He taught me the basics of Christian living, worship, prayer, reading the bible, learning humility and being a servant by showing God's love to all.

I also must acknowledge that God wasn't the only Person who was patient! Several other key people in my life forgave my blunders of pride in my immaturity and helped me to push through to the next level of discipleship. I was a 'rough diamond', but they saw the potential beauty of the finished work of God shining through. I didn't want to waste time trying to be someone or something I was not.

By nature, I am a full on type of person and I had wasted enough years of my life in selfish and foolish endeavours. I was determined to be transformed and follow the Holy Spirit's direction to put God first, others next, and myself last. Sometimes I got it right, and other times I failed miserably, but I believed God loved the fact I was at least trying.

# The Birth Of A Worshipper

## Worship and the word

It was my habit to turn up at meetings desperate to sing love songs to Jesus because when I sang to Him He poured out His love on me. I arrived empty and left full. I thought you had to go to a church building for that to happen until one life changing night I heard a man teach about worship. It blew me away! He said that you should not come to a meeting just to get something from God, but that you ought to come prepared to give something to God from your own heart. I loved it. It made such perfect sense. I didn't want to be a selfish worshipper but an extravagant one. I purposed from that moment on, that I would worship God with all of my life. It would be several more years before the phrase 24-7 meant anything to me, but this revelation about worship was another moment when heaven touched earth and changed me forever!

My home became a place where I could sing, dance, and think about God. I had no Christian worship music but I just improvised and sang the songs of gratitude in my heart. I lost hours and days and weeks in wonder at His perfect being. I would fall asleep thinking about Him, and waken again thinking about Him in the morning.

During this period, my mind slipped back into childhood remembrances of Sunday mornings in a traditional Presbyterian Kirk. I loved to sing the hymns from the old church hymnbook. I sang them until I was dizzy and out of breath. God had revealed His power to me even though I couldn't qualify it as such at the time. The pews were wooden and uncomfortable but God met faithfully with me each week. When Communion rolled around, the beautiful crisp white linen that swathed the pews bedazzled me. The silver platters of bread and the crystal wine goblets spoke deeply to my heart of the majesty of the God, His purity revealed to my child's eyes through the spotless linen.

In my new lifestyle of worship, I began to study my Bible. I wanted to know all I could about God and I felt the Book He had authored would give me access to His personality. I bought study notes from a local Christian bookstore, but most of these used language from another planet. I had no background to be able to decipher the Christian phrases, and I was overwhelmed. I gave up on them and asked the Holy Spirit to help me read the Bible instead. Without being taught, I simply knew the Holy Spirit loved to reveal truth about Jesus and Father. I committed to spending time reading the scriptures and praying through things God bring to my mind. It wasn't a structured Word study. Sometimes I couldn't get into it. I would open the pages, read the words, wonder what it was all about, and then give up!

At other times, the pages came alive to me and I marvelled at its stories of Life and Death. My mind filled up with images of God that caused me to be in awe of His majesty. He was the Mighty Man on the cross, who was also my Majestic Father, my friend and the Creator of the Universe. When I was a little girl, I had thought he was an angry God who dealt severely with sinners. Some people I knew thought he was a God of love who could not get angry. In my mind a picture was forming that was between these two distorted images. God was healing me from fear and showing me the beauty of respecting and honouring Him through a lifestyle of worship. I think that was when I began to both love and fear Him. It was a safe place to shelter from the storms in my soul.

### His majesty

I was in a season of total focused worship. I was lovesick for my king, and could hardly wait for each new day to begin so that I could get up and dance and sing love songs to Jesus. This particular day I spent three hours in the morning with Him, and by the end of that time, there was just silence filled with the sweet heavy presence of Christ. I lay on the floor with my eyes closed, happy tears spilling out on to my cheeks.

Later that day, I sat down to read a book, but it was impossible to concentrate. The Holy Spirit was drawing me to spend that time with my Saviour. I gently heard the whisper of His voice saying, *"Come"*. I was undecided to begin with, but eventually I chose fellowship with my Sacred Friend and softly began to sing from a grateful heart for his love and Grace. My soul cried out, "His Majesty, His Majesty, His Majesty."

With those words, the Lord opened the heavens revealing a vision of His throne. One moment I was home worshipping, the next my spirit was transported to Heaven to observe the Lord in all His Majesty. Wondrously, I was able to see Jesus as Holy King in all His Glory. The throne was purest gold and shone more brightly than the stars that light up the universe. A sapphire blue sea surrounded the throne. It reminded me of the sapphire path of God's presence that Moses and the elders walked along as they went up to meet Him on a mountain long ago. In the middle of this thought, I was captivated by the sight and sound of the twenty-four elders as they fell face down before their great King in loving worship. They were in circles of eight, the first eight forming the inner circle positioned at the Lord's feet. The next eight formed a circle with the remaining eight doing the same

The elders threw down their golden crowns at the Lord's feet over, and over again, bowing before Him in reverent worship. As this seemingly unending process continued, they sang, "Holy, Holy, Holy is the Lamb of God." The winged creatures dutifully guarded the throne watching over his Majesty, whilst winged cherubim acted as guardians of the Ark of the Covenant. The golden Ark was placed before the Lord and worship in heaven escalated to a breathtaking crescendo.

On Jesus' head were many crowns and holy power radiated from His being. It was impossible not to worship the One who created the heavens and the earth. I joined with the angels in singing, "Crown Him with many crowns." This proclamation continued for some time and I stood in awe, marvelling at the mystery of knowing Christ as my Saviour, my King and my Friend. I was consumed with passion for Him and wanted nothing more in this moment.

The Lord was being transformed from glory to glory as the worship continued. His eyes became like flames of fire and out of his mouth came a sharp two-edged sword as described in the book of Revelations. His hair was luminescent and flowing, appearing almost white with copper and auburn emanating from it. He looked terrifyingly beautiful and magnificent. I shook and trembled in the depth of my being. I saw Jesus as the Judge of all nations.

As I gazed on my Master, visions of future holy judgements began to appear before my eyes. It was as though I was looking into a time tunnel and could see into the past, the present and the future. I saw graven images and false gods from throughout history and Jesus destroyed every single one of them with the Rod of his authority. The sceptre of Christ's power caused the false gods to crumble.

In His holy presence, I became more and more aware of my own sins. Understanding began to dawn in my heart, that, there are many things that the Lord will judge as idolatrous. I began to thank Jesus for His mercy towards me and a wave of repentance flooded my being for the idols in my own life. Desire for recognition, greed, lust, reliance on money, hidden pride, all of these sins and more were before my King. I was appalled at the filthiness of my own heart compared to His purity. I was desperate to be pure just like Jesus, my High Priest.

I felt so unworthy to look upon Him in His majesty. All of heaven joined with one voice proclaiming, "All other gods of the nations are idols." I cried out in agreement with them emphatically declaring that Yahweh was the One True God. Part of me was petrified to look on the Holy One but my heart ached to the point of explosion to be near Him. In an instant, I was transported directly by the Lord's side.

I did not say one word and neither did I pray. I felt startled and overwhelmed by this unexpected gesture from the Lord, so much so, that initially I could not even muster the courage to look into Jesus' face.

The Lord watched patiently as I hesitated, then He gently turned my face toward His, and smiling, he lovingly kissed my cheek! It was the kiss of all kisses. Complete silence surrounded me as I nestled admiringly up to Jesus and expressed my love to Him. In this encounter of love, it was as if nothing else existed, except the sacrament and beauty of this Holy moment.

The Lord had been worshipped in all his glory and yet he heard the whisper of my heart's desire to be near him. He, momentarily, laid aside his Majesty to allow one of his own to come close to him. He lifted me right to his side tenderly placing a kiss on my cheek. I wept endless tears of joy at this expression of his love, grateful that I was wrapped, in his presence. I asked the Lord why he had allowed me this great privilege when, so often, I have neglected to make appropriate time for him, sometimes ignoring his gentle requests to join Him. I was stunned to realise that the Lord knew my heart so well that, even while all of heaven worshipped and adored him, he still could hear the longing of my heart, and call me to his side. Before I departed this wonderful place of communion, the Lord instructed me to receive and share these words:

He said,

*"Child, when you make time for Me, I make time for you. There is nothing in heaven or earth more precious to Me than when My children seek My face. I hear the faintest whisper of your heart to come to Me, and I am quick to answer. The angels understand that they are always in My Presence and they, along with all of heaven, step silently into the background each time a child of My heart approaches my throne. You may come boldly before My throne because of My blood. It is My love that draws you here and it is your willingness to come that allows you to be heard. Tell My church, all of My children, that I am waiting with an aching heart for moments to kiss each one and hold them in My arms with great tenderness"*. Amen.

# CHAPTER 8

## GLORY AND GROANING

I had seen King Jesus on his throne but that didn't mean everything was plain sailing back on planet earth. Our family finances took a serious hit and it took many months to sort out. Stephen has a genius intellect and is gifted with a keen business brain. He has always worked hard to provide for our family. Sometimes his genius has taken us on some mad career paths, and at times I've been almost demented with the never-ending stream of new entrepreneurial ideas and 'make it big' plans. Despite a few wild goose chases, Stephen is really talented and I love and respect his skill as a business strategist.

Unfortunately, after setting up his own (successful!) training business, two of Stephen's partners hijacked the company and temporarily ousted Stephen from his position as Managing Director. The bank accounts were frozen whilst a legal battle ensued. We found ourselves in a catch-twenty two situation with our finances. Although there was money in the bank we could not access it, and because we had money in the bank the State would not assist us. We were penniless and learned to pray in God's provision during this time.

It wasn't easy with a young family to support and there were days when our cupboards were empty and our hearts heavy with the responsibility of the house bills and the children to feed and clothe. God was gracious to provide for us, albeit the answer to prayer usually came at the eleventh hour! I sometimes wondered if God's clock was slow. Eventually Stephen regained control of his business and the matter was settled legally in his favour. Stephen's mum was a wonderful support during this period of our lives, and regularly brought us boxes filled with groceries. She also made major contributions towards our legal expenses.

Stephen drowned his sorrows and I felt isolated in my marriage. It was a lonely place and I pursued my relationship with Jesus with a renewed dependency and urgency. He was my friend and understood my pain when no one else could.

At church, I felt a bit like a duck out of water and wondered if there was somewhere I could go where I would fit in better. After several months of praying I moved from the Church of Scotland (where both Stephen and I were members) and transferred to another fellowship. Stephen didn't go, so I went alone. The next few months proved to be painful, but I learned precious lessons in humility and grace.

I was disappointed and surprised to find the new fellowship wasn't the place of religious freedom for which I longed. What I discovered was more like a prison, than a place of liberty for captives who had been set free. The control was a heavy weight on me. I was tired and didn't feel like a fight, so I stayed quiet and did as I was told. So much for the rebel of righteousness!

Initially, that involved modifying how I dressed and how I laughed. I was informed I was too loud and I didn't dress in an appropriate manner for a godly woman. Although the spirit in which those comments were made was harsh and abusive, there content was probably fairly accurate! My laughter has always been uproarious. I am told it is highly infectious. When my chuckle muscles get going, most people end up in fits of laughter with me. I once asked Jesus if I could have an elegant titter, to which He replied, *'No child, I gave you that humongous guffaw and it is a delight to my heart and brings joy to many.'* So the matter was settled – my laughter was loud and I needed to learn to deal with the fact that not everyone found it attractive.

Regarding the way I dressed - in truth something of the disco diva still influenced my wardrobe and although my will was not immediately submissive to suggestions to change, it wasn't long before I took a long hard look at the way I dressed. Out came a black plastic bin liner and in went half of my wardrobe! I threw out the sassy numbers, the slightly too low necklines and the over tight trousers. I didn't give up everything I liked, but the exercise made me focus in a positive way, on giving a godly impression through my outward appearance, as well as from my inner transformation. I tried hard to obey my leaders. One day I forgot about the control and started to dance in the church aisle. I had never danced in church before and I gave it all I had. It didn't go down well with the leadership. After being berated about the dancing and accused of attention seeking during worship, I apologised to the pastors, and asked Jesus to forgive me if I had taken an ounce of glory away from him. I was told that if I ever did anything like that again I would be banned from the church! The next week I turned up for church – no loud laughter and looking as respectable as I knew how. One pastor greeted me warmly and commended me for my humble response. I appreciated his kindness after the cruel remarks and the stern discipline, just for dancing.

I took my place and the worship commenced. In unbelief I watched the co-pastor start to dance. I looked around and every single person in the room was dancing except me. I couldn't believe my eyes. I thought God was making fun of me and I started to cry. He spoke with such tenderness to my heart, *"Child, last week you danced on your own. Today everyone will dance with you. This is my vindication. Now dance in honour of my Name."* I didn't need to be told twice and I danced on injustice thanking God he wasn't religious!

The dancing wasn't the only thing that got me into trouble! The prayers of the South African prophet were exploding in a prophetic flow that I didn't know how to handle. Without an inkling of spiritual protocol, God gave me the grace to understand that you can't just shoot off like a loose cannon on board a ship and that it is important to work with leaders and not against them. I was just learning to move in prophecy and I hadn't had any teaching. Everywhere I turned the Holy Spirit was speaking to me. I wrote down what he was showing me in pictures and visions. He also told me things about people, which I later discovered were called words of knowledge. I gave my notes to the pastors and asked them what I should do next. It was time for another disciplinary session.

### Words and warnings

To put it mildly my pastors went berserk at what I had submitted to them. They informed me that it was their opinion that if God was going to speak to their congregation it certainly wouldn't be through me, but that he would do so through them. They therefore dismissed the whole thing as being from the devil and told me to stop. I was utterly devastated and couldn't stop crying.

One of the words of knowledge I had submitted was a personal warning for the pastor. I had been really careful to offer the prophecy in a respectful way. In my immaturity I didn't realize that to warn a pastor of sexual sin, no matter how carefully it was couched, was like a match being lit in a dynamite factory! The result was explosive. I was severely disciplined and I felt terrified to open my mouth. It was like being a child again, confronted with an angry dad.

I sought the help of a few older ladies who were not connected with the fellowship. I trusted them, and they prayed with me and God restored my peace. A short while later, Stephen asked me to return to our local church. It was a relief. I left with the blessing of the pastors. Sadly, within a few months of my departure, the co-pastor fell into sexual sin, and his marriage collapsed. He left behind a trail of tears and a disillusioned family and congregation.

My family were noticing the changes in me. Even my husband remarked one day, 'You are not the woman I married.' It was true. I had changed so much and was on a collision course for yet more divine consensual transformation. For my words to be effective my faith had to be deeply lived. It bothered me that my mum, sister and brother didn't really know 'the real me'. I wasn't deliberately deceiving them; they just got embarrassed when I spoke about my faith. I longed for each of them to know Jesus' love and I made a decision to 'come out' of the Christian closet and be totally open and share my faith more fully with them. God helped me do this in a practical way but initially I didn't thank him for the persecution! My groans preceded His glory.

Our local newspaper was running a series of letters that were part of an ongoing debate about the financial demise of a local church.

I had followed this debate avidly and was horrified that money seemed to be the deciding factor on the future of whether a church remained open or closed down. I wrote a letter to the paper and they printed it, word for word, under a huge bold heading. Without realising I had written my first sermon.

I was stunned that the newspaper published it verbatim. I thought no more about it until I turned up at my mum's house for a coffee and general chinwag. Mum was not available for comment. The dear woman had been so affronted by my letter that she had to take to her bed with the shock of it all. I felt dreadful that mum was so upset, but didn't really think the circumstance merited such an intense response.

### Mad?

Things turned from cool to positively arctic and my family treated me with superior aloofness. My mum expressed her concerns to me about my mental health and wondered whether or not I had become involved in a cult, had been brainwashed, and, might be mentally ill. Sadly, my brother didn't speak to me for months afterwards. It was almost five years before this was comfortably resolved between us.

I was naturally upset and turned to a mature Christian woman for counsel. Her response was not what I had been expecting. Instead of being sympathetic to my hurt feelings, she told me to put myself in their shoes and try to understand that my family were just embarrassed and needed time to re-adjust to the 'new me'. I saw things from a more Christ like perspective after that. I was going to love them, no matter what. Eventually my prayers and patience paid off, and mum and I had a really open conversation about my faith and what it meant to me. I was able to re-assure her that I was not insane, but was just genuinely in love with Christ.

# CHAPTER 9

## DIVINE ROMANCE

The persecution I experienced as a Christian caused me to fall more profoundly in love with Christ. He had delivered me from darkness and His light intoxicated me. My spiritual prostitution had been replaced by His purity. I loved much because I had been forgiven much. I enjoyed fellowship with God. Sometimes that involved simply sitting still, waiting at His feet (just like Mary) praying, reading my Bible or simply being with my Lord. Once I was reading about the time she had poured perfume on Jesus' head (*John 12 :1-8*) and I desperately wanted to emulate her love of Christ. I searched the house and found the most expensive bottle of perfume I had. I opened my bedroom window and poured out the whole bottle as a love gift to Jesus, praying all the while and wishing I could see Jesus face' and wipe His feet with my tears. I didn't tell anyone about the perfume and amazingly Stephen bought me a bottle of perfume just a few months later. It was a surprise gift from him – a bottle of Chanel No. 5 twice as big as the one I had ruined for love of Christ.

I tried to stay close to Jesus even when I was busy (like Martha); my heart was full of thoughts of Christ. He was never far from me. I lived, in the moment, with passion for my King. During my quiet time (a special time I set aside just to be with Jesus with as few interruptions as possible from the outside world), my thoughts were full of His presence. I couldn't think about anything else and neither did I want to. I began to imagine His beautiful face and gently called out His name over and over again. 'Jesus, Jesus, please come'. He answered me in a vision where I saw Him walking by a lake, placing lilies on its surface.

The vision was a metaphor about God and his children. Jesus spoke with me and affirmed that when we make right choices about personal lifestyle, it draws us in closer and deeper in relationship with God. In the vision the Lord compared His presence to a serene lake and then a peaceful ocean; later He painted a picture on my heart where believers are likened to lilies on the water! The lilies were extremely beautiful just like the loveliness of our hearts as they are changed to be Christ-like.

### The Shulammite (Song of Songs)

The Shulammite was a lowly shepherd girl who fell madly in love with a shepherd who was actually a king. She was just an ordinary girl getting on with her life. The shepherd king loved her just the way she was and found no fault in her amazing devotion to him; despite facing many difficult circumstances their love continued to grow deeper.

Her relationship with the shepherd king caused her to be despised and rejected by many. Even her family and friends mocked her and beat her for the sake of this love, but still she could not give him up. The more she knew him the more she loved him.

No one understood why she continued to love the shepherd king even after he disappeared for a short time. The shepherd girl kept searching for him and being apart from Him only made her love grow stronger. When they were eventually re-united he melted her heart with his gentle Love and he pursued her and won her for evermore. Eventually the two were married and the humble shepherd girl became a queen in the King's royal courts. Their love was unquenchable and beautiful beyond words. Some see the story of the Shepherd King and his Shulammite as an allegory of the love relationship between Jesus and his Bride (the church).

I was worshipping the Lord and I found my spirit transported to a most exquisite place. I saw the Lord by a beautiful pond, where he was tenderly placing lilies of infinite beauty upon its tranquil surface. I noticed that each of the magnificent blooms was white and had traces of silver and gold in their stamens and on their petals. The trumpets were perfectly formed and the flowers emitted a fragrance that was indescribable in its heavenly aroma – an echo of the essence of the Love of Jesus. The expression on the Lord's face was one of Fatherly pride and the deepest love and affection.

The water was a deep, azure blue and there was no hidden menace or undercurrent to it. It reflected the perfect Peace of the Saviour. I immediately understood that its depths were unfathomable, as it was a reflection of the One who sustains the Universe by his powerful Word. The tenderness of the Saviour surrounded this place and I felt absorbed in his beauty and peace. Unity permeated the atmosphere and grace, goodness and loving-kindness abounded.

I was keenly aware that there were relatively few lilies on the pond, and I sensed it was the Lord's desire and deep longing that many more would be placed there. I drew near to Jesus and gently asked him about the meaning of the lilies. He answered,

*"My precious child, this lake is called 'Serenity' and each of the lilies that I place on its tranquil surface represents a child of My own.*
*These are the ones who have searched after complete union with Me with*

all of their hearts and whose longing for the perfect union with My Spirit have taken them through many trials and tribulations, and who, like the Shulammite, have entered into a deep and blessed union with the Bridegroom.

I love all of my children, but those who desire complete and total owner-ship by Me may enter into an intimacy reserved for only those who are total-ly devoted to laying their self-lives upon the altar of heaven, to be made holy, as I am holy. This is the place of My perfect rest and joy (Luke 12:27-31). This is the place of totally abiding in Me. This is the place where strife comes to an end and the life of the flesh is crucified in Me. I long for each of My beautiful children to enter into this level of intimacy with Me. It is not for the select few but for all who will hear the call and who are willing to be co-crucified with Me."

### Another description (with the same Heartbeat!)

"My precious child, this lake is just like My loving presence that itself wraps around your heart when you are close to Me. It is calm and peaceful. You won't find trouble here. These lilies are just like you and the many oth-ers who have searched for Me with all their hearts, longing for intimacy with My Spirit. You have suffered and endured much for the sake of loving Me. Like the Shulammite you have not given up and My banner over you is Bridegroom love.

I love all of my children, and those who long wholly to be Mine may enter into a deep level of sacred friendship. This fellowship is reserved only for those who are willing to lay down their selfish ambitions, desires, dreams, wants and needs as a love offering. The altar of faith is the meeting place in your heart, where heaven touches earth and you are changed by My Spirit to be made like Me. You are declared sacred by My blood and set apart because I Am holy.

It is not easy for my children to lay down self-life. This involves the sur-render of body, will, mind and emotions. The natural inclination of the human heart is to self-rule, but self-determination must give itself over to My authority and control. Self-indulgence and selfishness must be replaced by compassion and consideration for others, for self-less actions are the hall-marks of a servant heart.

Mr dear children do not be discouraged for the process of surrender takes time. My Spirit will help you and you will find perfect rest and joy (Luke 12:27-31) when you live in Me. In obedience to My will, you will discover that anger and bitter disagreements will come to an end. I long for each of My beautiful children to enter into this level of intimacy with Me. It is not *just for a few but for all who will hear and are willing to embrace the lifestyle of Jesus – the joy and the suffering."*

### Back to the Original Version . . .

The Lord instructed me to lift my eyes and as I gazed into the horizon I saw an ocean as tranquil as the pond I had previously gazed upon, and on the ocean were millions of lilies. The Lord spoke to my heart and said this represented a day when all striving would cease when all of his children would enter into their promised rest in him, dwelling eternally in his Presence and Peace and Love – a picture of eternity.

# PART III

# THE CRAZY

*Crazy adj. 1. insane or unbalanced, especially as manifested in wild or aggressive behaviour 2. extremely enthusiastic about something 3. appearing absurdly out of place or unlikely.*

# CHAPTER 10

# LEARNING THE LINGO

It hadn't escaped my attention that God did amazing things when people prayed. I had first hand knowledge of this after being healed when other people prayed for me and I wanted to invest in others in a similar way. God knew how many times I had overcome and He taught me that broken hearts are made to hold His blessing (*Proverbs 17:22*). If prayer was a way to hear God's voice and release His will on earth, my loud response was, 'count me in!'

When I was a little girl I used to pray each night before going to bed. "Four corners to my bed, four angels round my head, Matthew, Mark, Luke and John, bless the bed that I lie on. God bless mummy, God bless daddy ..." This short devotion formed the basis of my childhood prayer life. It was repetitive but the simple act of reaching out to a big God had a 'feel good' factor to it. I concluded this was a sweet way to pray, but not deep. Aside from this, the only other type of prayers I experienced as a child were the Lord's prayer (*Mt 6:9-13*), which we learned to recite at school and the 'God, please help us', emergency kind uttered from fear stained lips.

I thought back to when I first met Jesus at age fifteen and remembered the intense way in which God had used me to pray for my father. Those were liquid prayers; tears that spilled out in the place of words. It was a powerful way to pray that God had validated by His Spirit. I discovered when the Holy Spirit moves through a surrendered heart on behalf of another, it's called intercession (*1 Timothy 2:1; Romans 8:26*). I looked around for other role models and was shocked and shaped by my discoveries. God used different people and tools to educate me, removing the religious hype and type along the way.

In our church, intercession was defined as the time when the minister prayed from the pulpit while everyone else lowered his or her head. There was no audible response from the congregation, just a silent agreement then the 'amen' concluding the minister prayers. This was meaningful but I couldn't connect in any deep way with God whilst it was happening. It felt moderately indifferent and a distant form of praying.

I attended various prayer meetings, keen to learn how to pray. I was intrigued that most prayer meetings were conducted in a circle of chairs, where people mumbled their prayers so quietly that I couldn't hear a word. My own style of praying at home was different to this.

I liked to walk about, sometimes I fell on my face, and occasionally my prayers were loud. I got quite emotional when I prayed. I cried when I thought of people who didn't know Jesus; I shouted when I got angry at the devil for robbing the vulnerable. I also liked to spend time just being with God. I noticed people around me were good at saying thank you prayers and making requests to the Lord (*1 Thessalonians 5:17*) and whilst these were all valid types of prayer, they lacked the intimacy of finding God and locking in to His heartbeat.

### Extreme enthusiasm for prayer

There had to be more! I was shocked by the apathy of many believers towards prayer. I discovered some people simply prayed out of habit; others prayed because they felt it was their duty. Some had a shopping list type approach to ask God for things. This didn't match up to what I thought God wanted for his children (*Luke 11:11-13*). I wondered when people would start asking God for his Spirit? The arrogance of youth reared its opinionated head once more, and I assumed I knew more about praying than the people I had encountered so far. Thankfully, my attitude improved quickly and I learned some respect for the genuine lovers of Jesus who had prayed faithfully for many years.

I caused offence when I asked how we could learn to pray more effectively. Most people dismissed my idea of learning to pray as preposterous. It didn't deter me. Jesus drew me into prayer like a magnet to metal. He was irresistible and so was the urge to pray. I prayed whenever I could. I hung out with people who said they wanted to pray. I met up with other young mothers and found a level of freedom of expression that I hadn't experienced in more formal church settings. I prayed on my own, with my children, and with any other Christians who would let me join them! I even began to step out and pray for people who were not Christians. All of it was new and much of it was nerve wracking.

I enjoyed praying on my own because it let me connect with my Father and hear his voice. My primary reason for praying wasn't to achieve an end result except that it was a key to intimacy with God. It was about relationship and not works (*John 15:7*) and I never tired of using my Saviour's name to pray (*John 14:13*). Jesus was my Intercessor (*Romans 8:36*) and, like Job, I wanted to say he was also my friend (*Job 16:20*) I discovered prayer was like a heavenly bank account – a safe place to make a deposit and one that carried the reward of divine interest (Matthew 6:6). I began to sow in prayer for other people (2 Corinthians 6:6), and this included the leaders who had ministered to me in my brokenness. Relationships developed out of prayer.

I loved and learned in the fruit these produced. God is good and kind.

## Strong foundations

God opened up the Word and gave me biblical foundations for the different emotions I was experiencing in prayer. When I asked about tears, he led me to (*Hebrews 5:7),* where Jesus is described as making his prayers and requests to God with tears and loud cries. When I wondered about the manifestation of laughter, God taught me of his supremacy and breakthrough anointing in *Psalm 2:8.* When I groaned and experienced birth like pains in prayer, he showed me to lean on him and allow the precious Spirit to pray through me (*Romans 8:26).* Most of the time God's commanded love was the motivator for my prayer life (*John 13:34, 35)* and I pursued purity, letting go of unforgiveness in my heart in case I blew my chances of divine approval! (*Matthew 18:35).*

I would be a liar to suggest my prayers were always God centred. This is an honest admission – I sometimes fell asleep in the middle of praying; a few times I even got bored and gave up before God was finished! Occasionally I prayed my own opinion thinking it was God's or I acted liked a hypocrite trying to amaze man with long-winded prayers. At times I prayed liked a heathen repeating phrases I thought sounded important, thinking I might impress God. I quickly learned this was not on if I seriously wanted to move God's heart in prayer. God love's a humble heart seeking his. I didn't need to pretend to be someone I was not.

I bought as many books as I could on the subject of prayer as well as pouring through Scripture. I watched videos and listened to teaching tapes about prayer. These mentored and encouraged me, inspiring me to go deeper in the arena of prayer. It was a relief to discover that I wasn't alone and other people enjoyed intercessory prayer too. I also discovered that God answers prayers of agreement from his children (*Matthew 18:19, 20)*

Eventually I met several people who called themselves 'intercessors.' I was a bit intimidated by their somewhat aggressive style of prayer, but they were kind to me and I learned more about the authority of Christ from them (*Colossians 1:18),* which was a foundation of greater trust in God (*John 14:1),* paving the way for future spiritual warfare. They ensured I knew about my spiritual armour (*Ephesians 6:18).* I appreciated their fellowship. A prayer leader got along side me and allowed me to ask a huge amount of questions, which helped to focus my thinking.

## Praying through the night

Whilst reading the bible one day I noticed that Jesus spent whole nights awake praying to His Father. At times he would be alone (*Luke 6:12*), whilst at others he would be surrounded by crowds of people as he conducted all night prayer healing meetings. The 24-7 bug was planted in my spiritual DNA.

It wasn't long before I couldn't sleep through the night without being wakened at some point with a prayer burden. Getting up from the cosy duvet was not immediately attractive and if I was particularly tired, I would try and ignore the nudges of God, but then the burden to pray would become so intense that I had to get out of bed. In truth, I wasn't always so gallant and in the morning I would feel guilty if I had slept through without a prayerful response. My worshipful heart had to acknowledge that sometimes prayer is hard work.

When I did manage to be obedient to the nocturnal nudges of God, I paced back and forth across the floor until the prayer that was on the Lord's heart had left my lips and was sealed with heavens amen. I made tea and ate chocolate digestives to help me stay awake, whilst trying not to think about my divine divan. During the wee small hours I saw visions of people in all kinds of situations and from different cultural backgrounds. God gave me their names and specific information regarding their personal situations. It might be finances, help with relationships, persecution, a miracle, a healing, a prayer to prevent an accident, a prayer during an emergency – the list was endless. God knows our needs intimately and the Holy Spirit was faithful to lead me. I crossed the globe on the wings of prayer without ever getting on an aeroplane! The nighttime prayers carried a sense of urgency, but unlike my childhood SOS petitions, these flowed from faith and not fear.

One evening the Lord brought a young woman I knew to mind and asked me to pray for her protection from suicide. I thought this was a bit silly to be honest, and started to speak back to God. It was the first time I remember Him being strict with me (*Hebrews 12:10b*). He replied, '*Catherine if you keep asking questions I can't use you in this ministry. There will be times when you will know why I ask you to pray in a certain manner and there will likewise, be times when you will not know and you will simply have to obey.*'

I apologised sheepishly and lost the next hour in spiritual warfare for this young lady. The burden lifted as quickly as it had come and I thought no more about it until several weeks later the young woman's husband shared with us that his wife had attempted to commit suicide; he had walked into the bathroom just in time to stop her taking a huge handful of deadly pills. Not only was the suicide averted, but also she gave her heart to Jesus right there and then. It was a power-

# Learning The Lingo

ful lesson in obedience. I was glad to be on the prayer team with Jesus.

## Helping others find Jesus

My son Mark was the first person I led in the 'sinner's prayer', the day before Halloween in 1996. I had never done this before, and didn't have a ready prepared script. I followed the Spirit's leading and soon the angels in heaven were celebrating. Daniel invited Jesus to be Lord of his life in August '97 – after many months of questions and answers, he said his salvation prayer in a no-fuss manner as we sat in the car at a set of traffic lights waiting for the lights to change colour. The green light, for 'go' came on just as he said his 'amen'. Leading people to Jesus was in my blood. I could sense it, and I didn't want to stop!

I prayed for another guy who was terminally ill. His wife had died the year previously and he had a little girl. For around three months I prayed for Robert's salvation. Eventually a friend and I went to visit Robert in the hospice. I was astounded by the level of suffering I saw around me. Robert himself was obviously in extreme pain. He spent time talking with us and shared how he was more of Buddhist in his spiritual thinking than a Christian. I thought to myself, 'Holy Spirit you never told me that!' Michael and I told Robert about the Man Jesus and he was captivated. Before we left that night, heaven had a new resident.

When we prayed with Robert, I laid hands on him and asked Jesus to heal the cancer. I was dismayed to hear the next day that Robert fell out of bed and broke his leg. This dear man did not deserve that! Over the next few weeks, Robert shared his newfound faith with all those around him. His eight-year old daughter was the first person he led to the Lord. Robert did more in those few short weeks than many people do with a whole lifetime. He was my hero and I truly respected his courageous witness. Despite our prayers of faith, it was God's will to carry Robert home. I didn't understand it and accepted it with some reluctance when Robert died a couple of months later. I made a mental note – I hated cancer with a passion.

## A journal with Jesus

I began to journal my prayers and my faith grew each time I wrote about answered prayer (*Matthew 18:20,21*). I was discovering God really was a God of the impossible (*Luke 1:37*). I was faithful with the little things God asked of me and He began to give me more and more prayer assignments. I don't think there was any particular formula that I followed, just obedience, even when my knees were knocking and the only thing holding me up was God's grace and my tenacity.

I was invited to be part of international evangelist Suzette

Hattingh's inner core prayer team and I threw myself into praying for outreach meetings where thousands of people gathered to hear the gospel message. I was unable to physically 'go' but in prayer I was lifted up by the Holy Spirit and taken to those meetings where I regularly saw angels, demons and many miracles. It was a kaleidoscopic spiritual whirlwind as I was caught up in the presence of Jesus. I served Suzette for almost three years.

## Pioneering prayer initiatives

I pioneered new prayer meetings in our local area. One of the first meetings I initiated was prayer for school children. I had three great kids of my own and was keen to share the blessing of God's love with other children too. Out of this I linked up with a national organisation called the Schools Prayer Network and eventually God used this tiny step of faith to seed a future school prayer initiative for secondary school students, which is now run by the teenagers whom I started the group with. Not that it was always plain sailing!

When the group first started nearly all of those who turned up for the prayer meeting were non-Christian teenagers, with just a handful of Christians. My young friend Sarah was faithful to pioneer the project with me. We were blessed but perplexed. We didn't know what to do, so we gave them all Bibles, worship CD's and then shared the gospel message with them. I almost got thrown out of school on one particular occasion when I anointed a young lad with oil and prayed for healing. The boy wasn't a Christian but had agreed to let me pray with him. At the time I didn't know anything about school protocol – i.e. physical contact with children is frowned upon – but I knew the prayer of healing worked. (Jas 5:15) I had been fasting for a week for this boy and God was faithful to heal him from serious blackouts.

I also set up a prayer chain in our local fellowship, under the protective canopy of an elder and senior prayer co-ordinator. The prayer chain was simple and operated by means of a series of telephone calls. When a prayer issue arose the chain would be initiated by the first person calling the next person on the list to pass on the prayer request. We had the privilege of partnering the God of miracles. He saved a tiny immature baby whose lungs had collapsed when we prayed.

The Lord intervened for another young boy I had befriended at the local drop in centre. It was the dead of winter and he ran away from home after an argument with his parents, dressed only in a pair of boxer shorts. We set up non-stop prayer cover for the family and for the army of local volunteers who went out combing the local area with the police. The missing teenager found sanctuary in the ruins of an old church building, and when he was eventually discovered three days later, the doctors said it was a miracle he had survived and could not understand why he did not have frostbite – but we did!

I enrolled on the prayer lists of Tear Fund, Bible Network, Open Doors and other missionary organisations. I linked up with the local prison fellowship after being convinced by Paul's words in Hebrews *'Remember those in prison as if you were their fellow prisoners, and those who are mistreated as if you yourselves were suffering' (Heb 13:3)* and I embarked on prayer for the persecuted church and for prisoners and marvelled at the faith of saints who were martyred for love of Christ.

Reading about the lives of Watchman Nee and Rees Howells inspired me. Watchman Nee had spent the last twenty years of his life imprisoned by the People's Government in China for his faith. Rees Howells left school at twelve, was brought up in a mining village and learned to love the unlovely by giving sacrificially of his time, his resources and his prayers. He set up a bible college in Wales and he and his colleagues prayed throughout the war.

I was challenged by their heroic selflessness. I thought about their lives and the difference they made by standing up for what they believed in – amazing Grace in a world driven by hate and greed. I too was desperate to be a history maker for Jesus.

# CHAPTER 11

## SCOTLAND THE BRAVE!

God began speaking to me about nations, beginning with my homeland Scotland, whose people and land I hold with deep affection in my heart. Without having heard of spiritual mapping or research at this point, God assigned me a prayer project that involved both. It all began with a vision I had in 1996 of people walking in a crosswise way across Scotland. I asked the Lord what it meant and he replied that prayer was needed on the ancient battle sites of Scotland. His exact words were, *'Catherine, I want you to weep prayers of repentance where men bled the ground red.'*

I asked God to confirm if this was from him and he did this the next night, through a visiting speaker to our church who was part of the Evangelical Alliance. He implored us to pray for our nation. It was all the confirmation I needed. This kicked off four months of research, studying maps, writing to university professors, linking with national prayer leaders and generally lots of hard work. By the end of this time I had prepared a list of battle sites, with dates and prayer points. I eventually submitted these to the prayer network leaders of Scotland, who embraced me warmly into their midst.

I was stunned to learn that YWAM Scotland were organising a cross over walk in Scotland to pray on ancient battle sites and repent for past sins and that several significant prayer gatherings had already taken place on battle sites for the same purpose. I hadn't especially enjoyed the historical research or the mapping, but it was an excellent training ground. I was ecstatic when God confirmed through this chain of events that he is speaking all the time to everybody, and I was excited that I had been able to hear him accurately.

Almost two years later, I was delighted to be involved in a battle site repentance prayer gathering on the anniversary of the Battle of Falkirk. It was the fulfilment of those four long months of research and I was humbled to represent Scotland as we met to ask Jesus to unite the United Kingdom in His love.

### A Sword, some sheep and a vision for Scotland

On another occasion I was driving to meet an evangelist friend who was ministering in Dumfries, Scotland. I was motoring along the beautiful countryside, when, unexpectedly, I had an eyes wide-open vision of a huge sword suspended over the land. I nearly crashed the car. It was raining heavily and my windscreen wipers were on full pelt, so I hastily pulled into the side of the road. It wasn't my imagination – the sword was still there and God started to speak to me about Scotland. I quickly grabbed a piece of paper and a pen and wrote down what He said to me and what I asked Him. I was so engrossed in the experience that I forgot to turn my car headlights off.

About three quarters of an hour later, I tried to start the car engine but the battery had been drained of its power by the lights. I trudged to the nearest farmhouse in the pouring wet rain, where God provided practical help for me. The farmer's wife was kind and gave me hot tea to drink and spoke endlessly about her sheep, which she obviously adored. I hadn't a clue about sheep but I was grateful for the tea. The farmer called a friend who drove to my car and helped to start it with jump leads. I did eventually make the meeting and spend time with my friend. I sent the prophecy God had given me to an Internet list and it made its way into the hands of many Scottish leaders who took time to pray and test the word. The feedback was extremely positive and I was tremendously encouraged.

### Vision - "Fire over Scotland"

The vision began with the Lord's sword descending from heaven. The tip of the sword was a flame, and the Lord took his sword and passed it over the land. As the Lord's sword swept the land I saw fire break out in every place. There were small fires everywhere. I could see fire on the hills, and I cried to the Lord, *"Is this revival fire, Father?"*

He replied, *"Child, this is the first fire I will send to Scotland. This is a fire that is for the Body. This is a fire that will cleanse and will purge and will winnow. This is a fire that will separate the wheat from the chaff, for this is a fire of my Holiness. For I have destined this nation to be a nation of holy warriors and I am refining and restoring My people. Many will oppose this fire in pride and bigotry, but know that it is I, and this is a necessary work of Holiness."*

Flood water then swept across the land and every fire was extinguished and I cried with a broken heart, *"Lord, the fires have all gone out, does this mean we've missed your visitation?"*

But the Lord answered, *"Child, this is a flood that I am permitting, do not lose heart. This is a time of testing for my children, but know just as the enemy desires to come in like a flood and put out the fires of revival, all this shall achieve is the raising of My standard of holiness above this nation. For I have heard the earnest prayers of My children, and they have moved My heart to compassion. This flood will reveal My people to be broken and hum-*

ble and contrite, and know this My precious Scotland, this is what I esteem. But you must rise up out of worthlessness and rejection and put on the garments of Righteousness and Holiness that I have prepared for you."

Then the vision changed again, and I saw men, women and children all over the land – in the valleys and on the high places, and as each of them spoke and opened their mouths, a flame of fire shot forth and I cried to the Lord, *"Lord, is this revival fire?"*

He said, *"Yes, child this is the fire of My presence that will touch the hearts of all those who will listen. I will use men, women and children who have come through the fire of My refining, who have understood My holiness. I will use them to reach the lost in this nation".*

And I heard a new and awesome sound of worship coming from the hilltops, a uniquely Scottish sound, and I saw demons running from the high places and as I looked below the valleys were full of people on their knees weeping and repenting before God, and I saw many angels ministering to the lost.

And I knew that salvation had come to our land. And I look up and was lifted by the Spirit of God to see one dazzling flame over Scotland. It consumed not, for it was the presence of the living God and I heard the Lord say, *"Child, I have established My holiness in this nation, and I have answered the heart's cry of My children. This is My eternal Presence that shall not be taken from the faithful."* Amen

**National and international prayer links**

The links with the prayer networks led to invitations to join prayer gatherings for the nation. Ultimately I was invited to the British and Irish Prayer leaders meeting two years later in January '99. I drove to Carberry Towers, Edinburgh and almost lost my nerve. I began to weep and the old feelings of inadequacy threatened to engulf me. I said to God, 'I shouldn't be here, I don't belong with all these important people; why am I here?' to which he replied, *'Child you are here because I called you, now go in and trust Me for all of your needs.'*

It was a profound time of blessing and I was delighted to meet up with men and women whom I really admired and respected. From this, links were forged with Brian Mills of the World Prayer Advisory Council and with Roger and Sue Mitchell, Passion. It has been my joy to support both of these ministries in prayer since that time and to be blessed as the relationships have deepened.

**Rally sprinter – run the race – a call to prayer**

Before I was even fully awake one morning, the Holy Spirit was already waiting to talk to me. I was somewhere between thinking about turning over for another forty winks and my feet actually hitting the floor when, in my mind I saw the Lord's hand. He was tight-ening a screw on a brand new racing bike. I took a closer look and saw he was fitting a shiny bell to it. The bike was a brilliant red colour and the crimson of the metal made me reflect on Jesus' blood sacrifice at Calvary and of his amazing love for all mankind.

The Lord tightened screws and applied a spanner to various bolts, with precision skill in the adjustments. He pumped air into the tyres and polished the spokes of the wheels, which shone brilliantly. By the time he had finished the tyres were perfectly balanced, and the rubber looked ready to hit the road. The seat was positioned to optimise trav-el conditions for the rider. It looked both comfortable and safe. Coloured ribbons were attached to the handlebars and I imagined how brilliant they would look blowing in the wind. The finishing touch on the bike was the name, which Jesus wrote in bold gold let-ters on the frame, *RALLY SPRINTER*. It rocked!

Jesus turned to me and smiled. He explained that the vision was a picture message (a prophecy) to call people in every nation to prayer. The bike speaks of that prayer journey with Jesus, and his desire for many more believers to join him. The bike had no basket and this means we are to empty ourselves of the world and rely on Christ for our every need. The air in the tyres speaks of God's breath, the Holy Spirit, in us and the balanced wheels symbolise the need for us to be in right relationship with God because when we give priori-ty to our relationship with Jesus, we are perfectly aligned with our Father's will. The ribbons represent Jesus power being released in prayer in His name by the church. Knowing Christ's absolute author-ity over all things created puts the devil in his place – under Jesus' feet and ours! There are some who are called to be forerunners, and will answer this rally call to intercession immediately. They will make a way for others to come after. It doesn't matter whether you are a fore-runner or one who will follow on later because Jesus needs us all.

The Lord then showed me who the rider was to be. He turned to me and smiled and said, "*It's you*" Incredulous, I replied "Me?? No way!" We laughed out loud together. It's been years since I rode a bike and I am not a sporty person at all. The Lord smiled with deep affec-tion and said "*Child, it's not about your capability, it's about your willing-ness to be obedient. I am your sufficiency and in Me all things are possible, all I am looking for is a yielded heart.*" With this Jesus took me by the hand and helped me to get on the bike. We are each personally called and equipped by the Father's hand.

I was carefully dressed in a helmet and knee/elbow pads – I'd like to tell you that I didn't argue, but I did. I protested, "But Lord, I don't want to wear that silly looking helmet and pads". The Lord explained that I could not go on this journey without his divine protection. Similarly, our spiritual armour *(Ephesians 6)* helps to protect us as we journey with Jesus. I began to understand that in like manner the 'joints' of the Body (the church) must also be protected and must learn to work together, particularly during a global call to prayer. The devil seeks to destroy the unity of the Body because unity is a key to unlock God's blessing *(Psalm 133)*. The helmet further spoke of protection of our minds, and of our ability to focus on Jesus during this prayer journey so that His thoughts will fill our hearts and our mouths will be full of His glory. Then we will be anointed to pray as holy heaven sent warriors of Love.

The final piece of protection was a pair of sunglasses. I liked these; they were cool! However, this was not the reason I was to wear them. It is not about our reputation, it is about God's. The glasses would help keep my vision clear and free from distractions, helping to keep my heart pure. Finally, I found myself racing along the road at great speed, bell ringing, and ribbons blowing. It was such a joy rush! I was totally focussed on Jesus and knew no fear. When we obey Christ He gives us His peace and the gift of the precious Holy Spirit. It's not about works, but surrender.

At last I saw the finish line approaching, and standing there waiting for me was Jesus, His face lit up with Fatherly pride. I finished the race and ran into His open arms, losing myself in His loving embrace. Tears of joy ran down both our faces and the Lord handed me a gold trophy. Jesus calls each of us to finish the race. It is love of Jesus that compels us to continue and to persevere. The prize is Jesus. There is nothing that we take with us when we reach the 'finish line' other than that which we have built for eternity. It is only Jesus that will satisfy our hearts.

I finally noticed the angelic host who were all around applauding. Heaven has been with us all along, but all I have seen is Jesus. The angels assist us as we complete the Great Commission. We are not alone, and they along with the silent crowd of witnesses, long to see the Bride run into Her Lover's arms. Jesus is waiting – will you answer His call?

*"Beloved,*

*Hear my heart today and listen to what the Spirit is saying to the church, those who have ears to hear and eyes to see. I am coming soon. I will have a beautiful Bride and she will run into my loving arms, for there is nothing in heaven or earth that can separate her from my love.*

## Scotland The Brave!

*I place before each of you this day a rally call. Hear the trumpet in the nations. This call to intercession is a Last Days holy call. It is for those who will give themselves completely to My will and who will bring their yielded hearts. I require nothing more, only your willingness to run the race with Me. I will give you everything you need for the journey. There is nothing that I do not see, and there is no inadequacy in Me. I am your sufficiency. I desire that each of My children hear and respond to My call. I spent many hours on earth with My Father in the place of prayer. I desire that you follow me. Where I am there also will my servant be. Those who are my servants must also follow me. Follow me into death - die to your own desires, that you might also follow me into resurrection power. For if the seed falls to the ground and dies it produces many seeds. If you will die to your flesh, you will see the harvest of My Righteousness in your lives. Many shall come and find shelter in the branches of your tree. My Father is the Gardener and the fruit that the Spirit produces in your lives brings Him great joy. Those who display such fruit, do so for eternity, and those who display this fruit will ask in My name and receive the answer to their prayers, for the Father honours those who follow me and go where I go, and do as I do. You will bring the Father glory by displaying much fruit.*

*And my beloved, my resurrection power is coming, as you have never known it. "IT IS TIME", this is the sound from heaven. IT IS TIME! By my hand I have conquered the power of death, and by My hand I shall have for myself a beautiful Bride, for I have spoken and the prophets of old have spoken and my Spirit shall bring to pass that which the Father has decreed since time began. It is time for My Glory to break forth in the nations. IT IS TIME. It is time for My bride to walk in holiness and purity and Righteousness. It is time for humility and the calling forth of the Christ fruits, which will wreak havoc in the kingdom of darkness.*

*We are to be married. I am preparing My Church. Those who will run the race to completion will know the fullness of my favour and my joy. I give you my peace. I cover you in My wings, I give you my fellowship. My arms are wide open and my heart overflows with joy for each one of my precious children. There is nothing that you can do to win my affections for My love is freely given. Grace abounds and all I desire is that you open your hearts and yield to Me. I have loved you with an everlasting love and long to draw you to me. Come into My Presence, seek My face. Hear My heart beat, run the race. It is time. Run in such a way as to get the prize. Everyone who competes in the games goes into strict training. They do it to get a crown that will not last; but we do it to get a crown that will last for ever."*

1Cor 9:24, 25

# CHAPTER 12

## I'M NOT A SPIRITUAL SNOB

Being involved with national and international prayer leaders didn't make me a spiritual snob! Deep in my heart God had seeded a vision for transformation of my life and others. I implicitly understood there is a time to pray and a time to act. As God had intended, faith and action were inseparable to me. One of the signs that Jesus is your Lord is to have a heart to serve others. Jesus of Nazareth likes to get close to people and spending time with Him has a knock on effect!

God just kept pouring His amazing love into my life and I got to the point where I couldn't help but share it with others who didn't know Him. A new level of faith took my feet to the streets and God got to invade my space 'big time'. There was no way I was going to stand on a corner and preach, so I opted for less intimidating encounters with people on a one to one basis. Trips to the café, the supermarket, the hairdresser, in fact any place I went, God was there waiting to express His heart. This caused me to feel sick with nerves as my knees shook and the saliva in my mouth dried up. Mostly this just happened without me giving it too much thought, although it often looked haphazard and crazy. It wasn't that I planned the encounters – God did. He set them up and sometimes I responded. There were still times when I couldn't pluck up the courage to speak to strangers, despite my love for Christ. It never failed to surprise me how hard it was to do such a simple thing, yet how easy it seemed afterward.

One cold winter night I was on my way home from visiting a friend. I didn't have a mobile 'phone and it was late, around 11.15 p.m. I took my usual route and along the way I noticed a man being brutally beaten by two men who were kicking him and pounding his head and chest off the concrete. The pavement was covered with his blood. Not being street-wise I pulled up to the side of the kerb (sidewalk), rolled down the car window and said, "Excuse me, will you please stop hitting that man?" The men stopped for a moment, looked at me as though I was completely nuts, then returned to beating their victim with renewed vigour.

I really wanted to help but was unsure about what to do next. The men were ferocious and they frightened me. The street was deserted and silent except for the muffled screams of the wounded man, but with each painful blow I became more determined to come to his aid. I parked the car, ran into a local Public Bar and asked if I could use the telephone to call the police. I was told, "No way hen, yer no phonin the polis fae here". Roughly translated, that meant I wasn't allowed to use the telephone and no one was willing to help!

In desperation I ran out of the Pub and into the Taxi Office next door, and begged them to help. Finally, two men got to their feet and ran with me out onto the streets. The attackers had run off leaving their victim for dead. I got down on the pavement, and held his bleeding head in my lap. I wept tears of compassion for him, praying and asking Jesus to come and heal and save him. It wasn't an eloquent prayer as the cold wind and rain lashed at his open flesh, but it was sincere. Eventually the ambulance and police arrived. I gave a statement and feeling exhausted, soaked through and freezing cold, fell into my car and started to drive home.

Unbelievably, after a few moments, I found myself caught up in a high-speed car chase. The two thugs had followed me! I am a terrible driver; I typically call cars by their colour rather than their make and model, and apart from putting fuel in them I really wouldn't know the back from the front if it wasn't for the steering wheel pointing me in the right direction! All of this to say, I am not equipped to be a high-speed driver. Pathetic, eh? I sang loudly in warfare tongues and cried out to God to help me. I drove like a professional racing car driver and took s-bends with unflinching accuracy. I am sure an angel drove my car that night, and helped me to shake off my attackers and arrive home safely with not a single hair on my now somewhat dishevelled head harmed. It was really late when I finally fell in to Stephen's loving arms, weeping uncontrollably and muttering incoherently, until I was able to articulate what had just unfolded.

The next day, I called the Police Station. I had been up for most of the night, praying for the victim. I discovered he had been taken to hospital but the Sergeant on duty said, "He was our worst customer last night". Confused, I asked what he meant. Apparently when the man re-gained consciousness and was interviewed by the police, he said that he had fallen down and would not identify his attackers. The policeman said the victim had been seriously injured and would be in hospital for some time. I was grateful to know he was alive and that in some small way I had helped him on the road to recovery.

For several days I prayed for the nameless man. After a while, the Holy Spirit very gently asked me a question that blew me away. He said, *"Catherine, when are you going to pray for the other men?"* I was shocked at my own lack of compassion. I had been so short sighted. The Lord then said, *"Catherine, I love the other two men, as much as I love the man who was beaten, as much as I love you, now pray for them all"*. I fell to my knees, instantly repentant for my lack of prayer on their behalf, and prayed for their salvation too.

I learned many lessons that night, most of all, my Father's heart for abuser and abused. If I ever find myself in a similar situation again, I won't be making polite requests to would be attackers. Instead, I will use my God-given authority and command the devil to stop his work in Jesus name. When I told a friend what had happened, she smiled and said, "Catherine, I think God gave you many angels". I smiled. I think my heavenly Father smiled too.

### Prayer leads to serving

Jesus was teaching me to love the unlovely. In truth, I didn't always like it and being God's messenger didn't look the way I thought it would. The more time I spent with Jesus the more I prayed. The more I prayed the more I seemed to bump into people who needed his love.

Once I was eating bacon, egg and chips with my children and the Lord asked me to go and pray with a couple that were sitting opposite me in the café. At the time I didn't much feel like moving. I was tired and didn't feel particularly 'anointed' and the children were fidgeting as small people often do. However, despite my unwilling flesh, I obeyed the Holy Spirit.

I walked over somewhat reluctantly to the couple and asked if I could pray for them. They said yes, and as I got down on my knees, Father's magnificent love poured out of my mouth and cascaded down on them. By the end of the prayer they were crying tears of joy. It was an uncomplicated prayer but it had a profound effect. The man said, 'Lass, you'll never know how much we needed to hear there is a God that loves us.' My heart was simultaneously filled with gratitude and conviction. I had almost missed an opportunity to share the blessing of God's love. I was so glad that God had opened my eyes to see the need and had flooded the dingy café with his compassion.

### The drunk and the destitute

One afternoon while I was driving home, the Holy Spirit instructed me to take a different route from normal. I did as He asked and spotted a lady who was extremely drunk and in need of help. The poor woman had fallen over and her clothes were dishevelled, her tights torn and her skirt pulled over her waist. I parked the car, helped her to her feet and prayed with her right there. We walked together, and with my arm around her waist to support her, I shared God's concern and care for her. Even in the depths of her drunkenness, her spirit connected with the Lord. I could see it in her eyes. His love had made a difference to her dignity.

# I'm Not A Spiritual Snob

I had lunch with a homeless man one day. He was sitting outside the bank when I visited the cash point. I asked if I could join him. We sat down together on the pavement and shared some sausage rolls and a cup of tea. He asked me if I would look after his dog for a few minutes. I was touched by his show of trust, because his dog was his only friend in the world. After a few minutes he returned and we started to chat. He asked me why I had sat down with him. I told him that I was a Christian and I thought that is what Jesus would have done. The stares of passers-by were directed more at me than my new friend. People seemed to be outraged by the incongruity before their eyes. My clothes were clean and fresh, his were dirty and smelly, yet I considered it an honour to sit with him for a while and share a simple meal and the profound love of Christ. Jesus taught me heart by heart, that prayer and mission go hand in hand.

## Vision: The nations overshadowed by Christ

During a time of prayer, I saw the nation of Scotland being overshadowed and raising my eyes towards heaven, I noticed the whole earth was gradually being overshadowed. I saw that the source of the shadow was Christ Himself, seated upon a white cloud with many legions of angels by His side. The picture was not that of a triumphal war procession, rather the meekness and majesty of Christ exuded from the heavenly realms, casting His glorious presence across the globe. I was compelled to stillness as I looked on His loveliness and experienced the refuge of the Lord's overshadowing manifest presence in a fresh way.

A banqueting table began to descend from the heavens towards the earth. There were, as yet, many empty places at the table. As it descended, countless invitation cards were also released, spiralling down to the earth along with the table itself. The cards were edged with gold and were a gracious invitation by our heavenly Father to attend the wedding feast of the Lamb.

The Lord directed my gaze back to the earth and I saw several different scenes. Some of the invitations landed directly in the hands of non-believers, who upon reading them were immediately spiritually awakened and came to a saving knowledge of the Lord Jesus Christ. I was amazed by this, until glancing to the right I saw that there were many millions on their knees praying that God would, in his sovereignty, touch non-believers in every nation on the face of the earth and understood that the invitations being delivered was an answer to united, Christ centred prayer for the lost. Other invitations were delivered into the hands of believers, some of whom received perhaps only one invitation to deliver, whilst others received many. These believers were then sent out to lost souls to hand-deliver the invitations.

Finally, I saw mercy trucks that were being filled with provisions such as food and clothing, and along side of these practical items there were also huge piles of the gold edged invitations inside the trucks too. These trucks were sent on mission trips to the poor and destitute and those who received the food and clothing also received the Master's invitation to the wedding supper of the Lamb.

The invitations that are shown in the vision are not literal pieces of paper, rather they represent the message of salvation through Jesus Christ, which will be inscribed on hearts that are/will be surrendered to His grace and compassionate mercy.

The vision speaks of the coming harvest of souls. The earth has never seen anything like it in terms of the speed at which nations will be simultaneously impacted by revival power. The message to the church is pray, prepare, get ready for the harvest, and GO! The overshadowing in the vision speaks of an impartation of power to the church to enable her to fulfil the great commission and the two great commandments.

### What does it mean to be "overshadowed by God?

The overshadowing of God speaks symbolically of God's protection (*Psalms 91, Isaiah 9:2, Isaiah 60:1-2, Mark 4:32, Luke 1:79*) and deliverance from demonic oppression and sickness, alongside of the release of miracles (*Acts 5:15*). To be overshadowed by God is to rest in the place of His refuge (*Psalms 91*) and to know him as a strong fortress and protection from the enemy of our souls.

Angelic encounters are often a part of the overshadowing process, as Mary the mother of Jesus discovered, when Gabriel appeared before her to announce his heavenly decree. As it was with Mary, so it is for every humble, yielded heart - the overshadowing process releases a deposit of faith and brings forth the ministry of Christ. *"For nothing is impossible with God" Luke 1:37*

The overshadowing process speaks of the fulfilment of God's promises (*Isaiah 38:8*) and is a sign of God's defence of His children. To be overshadowed is to know the faithfulness of God, the fear of the Lord and to receive His favour bestowed on faithful hearts. Hezekiah came to know the power of God over the very shadows themselves. His experience points to the brevity of life, the experience of death and contrastingly the eternal nature of God and His perfect plan of salvation. Hezekiah's life was prolonged by an additional fifteen years. He knew the mercy and compassion of God as He came to the defence of His people. (*2 Kings 20:9-11, Isaiah 38:8*)

To be overshadowed by the power of God is a transforming

process. One cannot help but be changed as the weighty glory of God descends on the earth. In the process of being overshadowed the voice of God is clearly heard, power is imparted on a residual and abiding level, the will of God is made clear and the manifest presence of the Godhead is gloriously revealed. The experience of overshadowing is life changing and permanent. The world is going to experience the overshadowing of God and the nations will be changed and saved according to His glorious riches in Christ Jesus.

# CHAPTER 13

# PROPHETIC BEGINNINGS

My son Mark learned to run before he could walk. One day just before his first birthday, he simply stood to his feet, squealed with delight and literally ran right across the lounge floor from one corner to the next. He had never taken a first step before this and in his excitement he ran as fast as his little legs could carry him. As his parent, it was absolutely wonderful to be a part of this significant moment of breakthrough in his life.

Having accomplished this amazing feat, he fell over and rolled about laughing. I did too and jumped for joy at my little boy's newfound discovery.

Despite the fact he had learned to run, Mark still had to master the art of balancing on his feet and learning to walk. I think my prophetic journey has been a lot like that too. I ran head first into the wonder of hearing God's voice and my response was immediate, but like my little boy discovering his gift, I had much to learn. I don't think I had even heard the word prophet or prophecy at this point. Initially, I just enjoyed the wonder of listening, speaking and living in God's voice without necessarily understanding much about the mechanics. In time, God developed my prophetic gift. He laid foundations in character and integrity and was gracious to teach me the language of prophecy and the posture of a prophetic heart along the way.

Hearing God's voice and learning how to respond to Him has been a journey of discovery. Through it all I've become more aware that Jesus' message, methods and ministry are extreme. Jesus was unpredictable. Crazy things happened through normal suggestions he made. 'Let's go fishing for men' turned into a mega harvest of souls that burst the proverbial nets (*Matthew4:19*); 'go ahead of me on the lake' revealed Jesus as the water walking God who could calm the waves and the wind (*Matthew 14:22*). 'Let's have breakfast', healed Peter's broken heart and saw him re-commissioned as a forerunner in the New Testament church (*John 21:12*) '*I am willing*' healed the leper (*Matthew 8:3, 4)* and raised the dead (*John 11 43*).

Through it all, Jesus taught his twelve disciples by sharing principles and showing them literal application of those core values through his lifestyle. Jesus mentored by what He did, what He said and how He lived. He used every day symbols to help people grasp deep truths. He mentored by assurance; He never bullied or intimidated and His authority was gentle but instantly recognisable. This same Jesus has been my Teacher. The Holy Spirit has granted me grace to co-operate and embrace invaluable kingdom lessons about the Voice of God.

## The woman at the well

Jesus once met a woman at a well (*John 4*). She was busy doing her own thing and had never heard of Jesus. He was thirsty and so was she, but she didn't know it until Jesus told her something about herself that He could not have known unless he was a prophet (*v16-19*). Jesus told the woman details about her life and it amazed her. As a result of these words of knowledge, the woman was able to connect personally with God. She totally forgot to do her own thing and started doing God's. She ran back to her village, told everyone she knew and met to *'come see a man who told me everything I ever did. Could this be the Christ? (v29)* No doubt some people thought she was mad, but many others believed her. They sent for the Man; He spent time with them and they were so impressed by His words that the whole community came to know God! Amazingly, this revival was sparked by one or two key pieces of shared information. The people in the town became worshippers because they experienced the reality of God's Love through the words of Jesus the Prophet.

I love this story because it looks a bit like my story too. It's the humdrum, ordinary routine of life and God in the midst of it all that makes it work for me. It's real and it's accessible. I wasn't looking for God but He found me. I didn't know God cared but He spoke personally to me and I became a trophy of his grace. God used an unknown woman at a well to save a whole town – He can use me too; at the core of every word there is something for everybody. One woman's blessing was multiplied into many. She was spiritually dull then awakened – so was I! The lady was willing to change and her response was immediate, so was mine. Jesus is not into stagnation; He is a God of change who does things differently. He bypassed her head, spoke to her heart and used her testimony to help shape a nation. When God began to be God in this woman's life she didn't have to pray for increase – the Lord does the adding when we actively obey Him. The woman at the well was willing to give everything she was for everything He is - and so am I. Are you?

## God speak

God was speaking to me and I began repeating what I heard Him saying or showing me in prayer pictures - apparently I was prophesying! Sometimes the Lord spoke to me while I was praying or worshipping. At other times I'd hear God's voice while I was washing dishes, changing nappies, running the children around to school or nursery, doing laundry or preparing the evening meal. It didn't matter what the activity was, God was in it if I was willing to give Him access.

People gave me descriptive labels for things I was doing. The prayer pictures were called visions and the explanation of the visions was known as interpretation. For an interpretation to be accurate, it was necessary to use discernment. Discernment is when you ask God for his counsel and wisdom on a matter. I was surprised at how much practise I needed to get it right.

I was eager to hear God's voice but in the early days I was probably keener to speak than listen. Over the last seven years the Lord has honed my listening skills. Being able to listen carefully to God is important for anyone who wants to learn about prophesy. I didn't always see pictures. Occasionally, I just opened my mouth and God 'stuff' came out in a gush of words that had a holy impetus all of their own. God used me to share personal words from his heart to others, in a similar way to Jesus with the woman at the well. When God did this people got healed, delivered, impassioned, released, commissioned, and personally revived. It was astonishing to watch as the Lord's words opened a heart.

### A spider and a birthday cake

I remember one of the first times the Lord gave me a word of knowledge. I was in a Christian meeting; a lady shared with the group that she was struggling with a phobia. She didn't say what the phobia was but asked if we would pray for her. I prayed silently and God showed me a picture of a spider and a birthday cake. I was not impressed, and felt like an idiot. Several minutes passed in silence. Five minutes became ten and eventually the leader of the meeting stood up and made a final plea for prayer insights. No one came forward. By this point, my heart was hammering so hard in my chest that I thought it would pop out of my rib cage. Shaking, I stood to my feet and awkwardly shared the picture of a spider and a birthday cake and then the Lord said to me, *'tell her I forgive her.'* I did this and the woman instantly collapsed and cried for fifteen minutes as God poured in His healing.

Once she was able to compose herself she shared her story. When she was a little girl she had played a practical trick on her sister. Whilst her sister was blowing out the candles on her birthday cake, the other sister threw a huge rubber spider at her. Tear and screams ensued. The father of the family was extremely angry with his daughter and her practical joke and decided to teach her a lesson. At an unexpected moment, he pushed the offending spider down the back of his daughter's t-shirt. It was such a traumatic moment for her, that she developed an immediate phobia of spiders and creepy crawlies. From that moment she had been plagued by feelings of condemnation, and a sense of inexplicable guilt had followed her until now. The simple picture of the spider and the birthday cake and one sentence from God changed her life and healed her pain. Despite the knee knocking which accompanied this prophetic experience, I decided words of knowledge were pretty cool and God could use me any time should He want to.

### Learning to walk

I tried to step out in faith each time God asked me to. Most of the time I was obedient, but occasionally I flunked out. I remember reading Cindy Jacob's book, 'The Voice of God' and praying the 'I'll go anywhere, do anything, say anything you ask Lord' prayer within its pages. I meant it with all my heart and just to be sure, God tested me within twenty-four hours!

On 3 August 1997 I was sitting in the pews of our local church not anticipating anything unusual. I prayed quietly for God's presence to come into the sanctuary. Quite unexpectedly during the worship, God spoke to me and I hurriedly scribbled down what He said on a scrap of paper. I wasn't sure what to do next, then the Lord said, *'submit it now.'* I thought ok Lord, but how? I had never seen anyone stand and share a prophesy during a Sunday morning service in the Church of Scotland. My mouth was dry and it felt as though I had a herd of elephants thundering around my stomach rather than fluttering butterflies.

I thought it would be a bad idea just to stand up and let rip. I reckoned someone more mature than me ought to read the words before I prophesied. I passed the prophecy to an elder sitting next to me and asked him if he would help. He read it, agreed it was from God, but then handed the paper back to me and said he wasn't willing to do anything about it. I was putting the paper in my pocket when the Holy Spirit spoke forcibly to my heart and said, *'Catherine, submit the word now.'* I stood up, walked to the front of the crowded church and approached the pulpit where another elder was preaching. I tiptoed up to him and whispered, 'it's a word from the Lord.' With a crimson face I stood there whilst he silently read the word. He then quietly folded it, gave it back to me and continued preaching. I returned to the pew, hung my head and wept.

A few of my tears were out of embarrassment, but for the most part I was broken hearted that the people in the church had missed an opportunity to be blessed. On this particular day the building was packed full of folks who do not usually come to church. At the end of the service I was finally able to submit the word to our minister's wife (our minister was off on sick leave at the time).

I went home, threw myself on the bed and cried for a long time. I ached for those who did not receive Father's loving words. I met with my minister a few days later and he affirmed the word was from God, and thanked me for my obedience to submit it.

*'There are many of you here who do not know me as a Father. I am a tri-generational God, I am the God of Abraham, Isaac and Jacob and I am your God. You have only known me from a distance. I am reaching out to you again, in these days I will return the hearts of the fathers to their children, and the hearts of the children to their fathers. I will reach down and put my saving arms around you. I am your Father in heaven and I know your needs intimately. You are my children and I have many gifts I want to share with you if you will but turn your eyes to me once more. For I am a God of the second chance, and I will never leave your or forsake you. I have kept a record of your tears and I will heal you of all that this world has wounded you with, but in obedience you must return to me, your Father in heaven. This day I proclaim my Fatherhood over you as a nation. Return to me my sons and daughters and take up your Godly inheritance.' (3.8.97)*

### Core values – love and servant-hood

God used this experience as a foundation block for my prophetic training. He was establishing important core values in my heart. Early in my journey I acknowledged that prophecy is a ministry of love (*1 Corinthians 14:1*) and servant-hood (*1 Corinthians 1:7,10*). Furthermore, as long as I was faithful to say, or do, whatever the Lord asked me, or go where He sent me, then the response of those receiving the prophetic word/action was not my responsibility.

God gives us the gifts of the Holy Spirit (*1 Corinthians 12*) as a blessing and to serve others with, but as I practised prophecy I noticed not everyone accepted the prophetic ministry in this manner. The reaction of believers varied from suspicion, fear and completely ignoring the words through to vehement denial. Sometimes people were only interested in 'getting a word' rather than having a personal encounter with God. They could be quite nasty if they didn't get what they were expecting. This hurt my heart and I didn't think prophets ought to be under such pressure to give personal 'predictions'. This looked too much like the psychic world I had left behind! On a more positive note others received the ministry in varying degrees from tolerance to acceptance and transformation. The prophetic brought encouragement, strength and comfort (*1 Corinthians 14:3*) to those who received it in faith. It was sometimes directive and usually specific. God is a God of detail!

These preparatory years were tough but blessed. I learned obedience and humility. I came to realise that the Lord will never ask us to walk through rejection or being misunderstood without first releasing His grace on our lives to overcome. Eventually study of the Scriptures along with life experiences revealed that persecution, misunderstanding, false accusation, rejection, and misrepresentation are part of the prophet's lot. What is wonderfully true is the greater blessing for enduring such headaches and heartache!

*"Blessed are you when people insult you, persecute you and falsely say all kinds of evil against you because of me. Rejoice and be glad, because great is your reward in heaven, for in the same way they persecuted the prophets who were before you.' Matthew 5:11,12*

### Spiritual gossip

I sometimes saw words written on people, as though someone had taken a marker pen and scrawled on their heads! I first noticed this on a weekend trip with my husband and children. We were eating lunch in a hotel when a young couple walked into the restaurant. I glanced at them and was horrified to see two words emblazoned on their foreheads. On the man I saw the word 'adulterer' whilst the woman bore the label 'liar'. I was shocked. I wondered if anyone else could see what I could.

Looking round, it didn't appear so. I went to the bathroom and asked the Holy Spirit what it was all about. He told me the couple were being unfaithful to their spouses and then He asked me to pray for their respective marriages, which I did. I told Stephen all about it. I told other people all about it too. I didn't realise I had just become a spiritual gossip.

God soon got hold of my conscience and sorted the problem out through the Scriptures. I was reading about Noah and his sons, after the rains, so to speak. (*Genesis 9:18-28*) Noah had planted his vineyard, tended his grapes and was now enjoying the harvest. Basically Noah drank too much of the new wine and conked out in his tent, minus his clothes. His son, Ham, being a bit of big mouth (ouch!) ran outside and told his other two brothers that their dad was naked and drunk. Shem and Japheth quickly came to their father's aid. Without a word they picked up a cloak, walked in backwards to where there father lay, and covered his nakedness. These boys had integrity!

When Noah awoke, no doubt with a throbbing head, he was sore at Ham and cursed him and his son for exposing his vulnerability! By the end of the story I was sobbing because I realised I had done just the same thing in respect to opening my mouth when I ought not to. God had shown me a vulnerable aspect about two other people. He had entrusted this informtion to me and asked me to pray for them. He didn't give me permission to speak to anyone else. I was so sorry for what I had done and was rightly gripped with remorse. I fully accepted the important lesson of praying a mercy filled response to God's divine disclosures regarding others. As the Lord has more firmly established Himself in my life, I have become a trusted confidant and over the years he has shared sensitive information about some extremely influential people with me and I hope I have proved myself a trustworthy servant.

### Timing – now, never, later

The Lord expanded my thinking to understand that timing is an important aspect of prophecy. The prophecy in my local church had been a 'do it now' word that was for sharing in that moment with a large group of people. The prophetic word regarding adultery was not for sharing. Some things are never to be disclosed; they are only to be prayed through one on one in private. There was a third aspect of timing in which God educated me. Waiting was the most difficult of the three to embrace. Like most young prophets in training, I was hopelessly impatient and thought everything was now or never, wrong or right.

In early 1997, I had a vision of people being baptised in the ocean near our home. It was so real I could smell the sea and almost touch the waves. The Lord gave me a prophecy to accompany the vision and instructed me it was to be prayed in the sea. I presumed I was to do it immediately but he said, *'No child, just wait'* . For six long months I asked Jesus nearly every single day, 'is it today Lord?' and the only answer I received was His silence. I kept on asking and to my frustration God remained silent. I realise now God wasn't ignoring me; He was teaching me patience and dealing with my presumption.

I had almost forgotten about the vision and the prayer when one cold day the following January, the Lord broke His silence on the matter and said *'it's time Catherine'*. He wanted me to go to the beach, get in the sea and say the prayer. Suddenly it all seemed exceptionally unattractive. My stubborn streak surfaced and I argued with the Lord, saying I had changed my mind and I didn't want to do it and could He please just find someone else? As with all my arguments with God, the best Man won.

Part of my reluctance stemmed from pride. I didn't want anyone to see me and ask what I was doing. At this point I hadn't read much about the major prophets in the bible. I didn't know that for these men, prophetic actions were a normal part of their lives. I thought the whole thing was a bit silly, but God insisted on getting in to the water to pray.

My husband, our three children and two friends headed off to the beach. Stephen said to me, 'I don't really understand what you are doing Catherine, but I can see that you really believe God wants you to do this, so I'll stand with you.' I loved him for that. I would have preferred a bit more enthusiasm, but Stephen's silent support was better than loud disapproval.

The water was perishing. I got in up to my thighs and thought, 'that's far enough.' At this point, the anointing of God took over and I was hidden in God's mighty presence. I raised my hands to heaven and boldly proclaimed the message He had given me almost a year beforehand - that many would come and be baptised in these waters to bring glory to His name. It was freezing but my heart was on fire with passion for Jesus.

When I got out the water my legs were blue. Stephen wrapped me in a beach towel and rubbed my icy limbs until the blood started to flow back in to them. He helped me put on dry clothes and my socks and boots. I was so cold and numb that I was unable to dress myself.

To date, I haven't seen anyone baptised in that particular ocean yet. However, I had the privilege of seeing six people give their hearts to Jesus, the night I was baptised. I turned up to see my friend get baptised and ended up in the tank myself! It's a long story, but suffice to say it was quite unforeseen. My 'surprise baptism' in May 2001 required radical obedience, which released sweeping anointing. It was another of those major kingdom moments in my life.

## Prophetic actions

I was keen to understand more about prophetic acts. By way of an answer I was led to study Ezekiel, Jeremiah and Isaiah, three of the major prophets of the Old Testament. I was amazed by my findings. These guys were off the scale in the bizarre things they enacted to bring home a prophetic point to the people of their day. God once told Jeremiah to buy a linen belt and wear it around his waist (*Jeremiah 13*). Then he told Jeremiah to go and bury it. He complied (with a lot less fuss than I had!) When he retrieved it some time later it was ruined. God spoke prophetically to Jeremiah and said that if the people of Judah and Jerusalem didn't give up their stubborn ways and pride, they would be ruined just like the belt. God also said that in the same way a belt is wrapped around your waist, so He had bound the people to him.

In my opinion, Ezekiel has to be the craziest prophetic dude in the bible. Ezekiel's prophetic acts were seriously sacrificial! His instructions from God included eating a scroll just before being sent to bring God's words to Israel, tying himself with ropes then being made silent by the Lord (*Ezekiel 3*), enacting the siege of Jerusalem, lying on his left side for 390 days to symbolise bearing the sins of Israel and lying on his right side for 40 days for the sins of Judah (*Ezekiel 4*). There were many more equally disturbing things the Lord asked of Ezekiel, each of which the Lord used to speak to Israel. Ezekiel's life was a living prophecy. The Israelites just had to look at what Ezekiel was doing in order to understand what God was saying to their nation. Ezekiel's reward was unparalleled intimacy with God. He had visions of the living God and was regularly lifted up in the Spirit to come face to face with the Lord.

Studying these men of God led me to this conclusion - a sign plus interpretation equals prophecy. When prophetic actions are understood, then they can bring edification to the whole church (*1 Corinthians 14:24*)

## CHAPTER 14

## THE INTERNET

In July 1997, I submitted my first prophetic article to Steve Shultz at the Elijah list. Steve was, and continues to be, the moderator of this prophetic Internet word list, which had around 10,000 subscribers at that time. Today the subscriptions have grown globally to approximately 70,000 and Steve and I have become firm friends and comrades in Christ. The prophetic article was a powerful vision and I was excited by the word and the response I received from people all around the world mirrored my own reaction.

### 'Arrows' vision

On the morning of Monday, 27 July 1997, the Lord awakened me with a vision of many archers upon a wall. The wall seemed to span to the ends of the earth. The number of archers was too many to be counted and went on as far as the eye could see. I knew immediately that this was a holy army, raised by the Lord's hand and that it was the first time so many had been called to this place. There was a hushed expectation as the archers waited on the Lord. The bowmen were pointing into the nations - every nation on the face of the earth was within striking distances of their arrows. There were also legions of angels poised in this moment of silence, before the Lord gave His command.

*The Lord spoke, "I am raising up an army of archers, the quivers from My bow, the sons of My Righteousness. They will fire My Word from the watchtowers and My Word will rain upon the nations, for I am doing a new thing",* says the Lord. *"We are entering a new phase of warfare".*

*"For I have sent the snow and rain to water the earth and to bring forth seed for the sower and bread for the eater. But now I am sending forth My Word, which is an unending and a mighty River. These are days when you will see the desert places bloom - if you will but ask in faith, believe in faith and receive in faith".*

*'Seek not a name for this new move of My Spirit. It is neither third wave nor new wave – it is My Kingdom come",* says the Lord. *"Just preach My Kingdom come, My will be done on earth as it is in Heaven and believe that I am coming again for My people. Heal the sick, raise the dead, cast out demons and proclaim that My Kingdom is at hand: for I am nearer than I have ever been before. Look after the widows and the orphans. This is my sover-*

eign Word to you My people – when you ignore the widows and the orphans you profane My Holy Name by this action. Feed the hungry and clothe those who are naked, for surely in these days I have given you every means by which you might meet their needs."

"Come together under My covenant, come into My temple, bring the multitudes with you that they might know my glory", says the Lord. "Tell them about their Father in heaven. Tell it to the fatherless children and tell it to the nations. Tell them I have known them since before they were born and I hold each one of them with tenderness upon My heart. Tell them that I am awaiting their homecoming with great joy. Speak to Jerusalem with tenderness."

"And as the darkness increases upon the earth know that I am increasing My Light, My presence. Take care that you live as children of the Light, let no part of you be in darkness lest you give the devil a foothold. For so long My children you have thought that this was about the sun setting on your anger. Look again into My Word and see that it is this and so much more. Put on My Virtue that I might reveal, by My Spirit, any unwholesomeness, and impurity, within your hearts. Do not become complacent in your salvation. Remember My precious children that you are deceived to the extent that you do not see things through My eyes."

"Look again to the cross. Look always to Me for direction, for inspiration and for confirmation. Let Me be your best expectation. If only more of you would truly lay down your lives for Me, truly nail 'self' to the cross, but so many of My children pay these words only lip service. There is fullness in Me that My Body has not yet attained and it is My deepest desire to pour Myself out upon you in far greater ways and measure. If only you would have the faith to ask, to ask for it My way, says the Lord, I wait for the men and women of faith to ask Me. That is all you have to do, is ask with faith in your hearts. Faith is not a test, it is My gift to you. Faith is not a trick, it is my eternal promise. Lay hold of it with all your hearts and ask in My name and I will be quick to answer. Lay aside the thinking of this world and look to Me for the desires of your heart."

"But you must first remember that you are to serve one another that the first shall be last and the last shall be first. Mean it with all of your heart when you say "for it is no longer I who lives, but Christ who lives in me." This will astound you in its fullest revelation."

"Know the seasons", says the Lord. "Learn about the Harvest.

*Understand that I must appoint heavenly workers for the field and also earthly workers for the field. Search again the Scriptures for My deep truths. Beware of false doctrine and bring all things into the light that they may be tested."*

*"Let the trumpet call go forth to every nation. Let the battle for the sons of Righteousness begin."*

And with this, the bowmen on the walls let loose wave after wave of living arrows, into the nations. The arrows represented the sons of Righteousness. They represented the sons of the living Lord. The Lord's word was going forth into the nations, and with each arrow there was an incredible burst of Light, a radiance of the Lord's presence. Angels were despatched along with each wave of arrows that was released. The earth was becoming so full of the Lord's glory – truly as the water of the oceans covers the sea; such was the Glory of the Lord being released into the nations. Never before has the Lord raised so many of His children to serve Him. Oh hear the word of the Lord sons and daughters and come forth for the King that He might send you as an arrow of His word into the nations.

## Communication explosion

Suddenly I was receiving e-mails from all around the world. People wrote to me and poured out their hearts. For several years I responded personally to each one. I invested a great deal of time in praying for people who contacted me and in blessing them as a prophetic servant of the Lord with a personal word. It was another aspect of my training and trusting in God, that even when people were strangers to me, God knew them personally. The fruit from this was bountiful. A number of key relationships have developed into Christ centred friendships and remain to this day. As well as this I was astounded when, without asking for it, God raised up a prayer shield for our family. People were volunteering to hold us up in prayer. We were humbled and delighted.

My writing was not limited to the Internet. In a flurry of prophetic activity, I also started to pray for a number of prominent leaders, both secular and Christian. One such leader was the British Prime Minister, Mr Tony Blair. In September 1997 I had a vision that involved Mr Blair. I typed it up and sent it off to 10 Downing Street. I offered to pray for Mr and Mrs Blair. I didn't hear anything from his office, so I called them and asked if the letter had been received! A few days later, I received a short note thanking me for my communication. I was very happy to have my note from the PM.

I sent many personal prophecies to UK and overseas church leaders. With each letter and personal prophecy I posted, I grew in faith. Sometimes they wrote back. One such note was sent to Pastors Ken and Lois Gott, Sunderland. They wrote back to me around four months later. The letter was kind and full of encouragement; they had been really blessed by what I had shared. Gerald Coates was another leader who thanked me for my letter and urged me to keep pressing in to maturity. It was so appreciated. I wrote to Pastor Dutch Sheets, USA and thanked him for writing 'Intercessory Prayer' a book, which really mentored me.

Sometimes leaders didn't write back. It took some time for the Lord to convince me that the reason for this was not personal and they were just extremely busy people. Maybe, for some, a reply was unnecessary. Once I conquered the enemy's latest 'rejection' attack, I plunged into more writing. My heart was to serve these precious men and women who had carved a path for the likes of me to walk along and it seemed appropriate to use the gift that God had given me as a means of blessing.

## Australia and Accountability

I enlisted on an Australian Internet list. I got to know various people through this endeavour and once again, invested time and prayer into the people I was networked with. Some of the articles I submitted to the Australian list were more teaching orientated than prophetic and I took my first steps into helping disciple other Christians whilst, at the same time, being discipled by those who were leaders of the list. I even got plugged into an on line prayer room where I would link up via the Internet with other women on a regular basis, when we would pray and prophesy over each other. I was glad that part of my secular training had been to learn to touch type at around 100 words a minute. My fingers could just about keep up with the Holy Spirit!

With all the new things going on in my life I wanted to ensure I had adequate accountability. Prophetic people need to be grounded in a local church as well as being in relationships that allow them to grow, whilst still being accountable. I believe in submission to leadership and with the increased level of responsibility I felt it was imperative to have mature people to ask for counsel. Endorsement by respected leaders and elders in the Body of Christ would also lend credibility to the prophetic words I was hearing from God.

After discussing the matter of accountability with my minister, he suggested that I look for someone with a national or international focus to help mentor me in prophecy. I set out to do just that with his approval. I didn't find anyone for a few months and panic began to set in. Where were all the spiritual mothers and fathers? After months of searching for a mentor, God put me in touch with a lovely English couple that took time out from their busy schedule to be of assistance to me. If I felt I had a word from the Lord, I typed it up and sent it to them for prayer input and assistance with the interpretation (which I sometimes got wrong).

The Lord used this relationship to buff a few edges of this rough diamond (removed 'to be sure' sounds like an Irish pun)! Tony was a direct man, and called a spade a spade. If he thought I had heard accurately from the Lord he totally affirmed it. Likewise, if he thought I was in error he told me that too – with no frills on. It was exactly what I needed, but I responded with prophetic tantrums, sulks and the occasional huff. Through Tony's keen insights the Lord was able to chisel away the critical edge on my interpretative skills. I worked through my perspective of rejection by continuing in the relationship and pursuing correction. Somewhere in it all I understood that it's about God's love whether I'm receiving His delight or His discipline.

## Israel

Tony worked tirelessly with many ministries in Israel. I didn't know much about Israel or the Jewish people, but the passion Tony displayed began to rub off on me. I recalled scenes of the holocaust I had watched years previously on television and my horror at the suffering of millions of innocent Jews. My heart was slightly stirred but I didn't think over much about it until the day I had a vision of the holocaust and then of a blood chilling mass grave in Czechoslovakia.

I wept a river for the poor souls who died nameless in this grave. God ignited a small flame of ardour for Israel, which He would one day turn into a furnace. On a family vacation to Bavaria, we had a sudden impulse to cross the border into Czechoslovakia. The guards took our passports from us and informed us we could not cross because our papers were not in order. I prayed silently in tongues. God came through and so did we. It was a small miracle to be in Czechoslovakia and I considered it an honour to worship and pray there.

# CHAPTER 15

# BLUNDERS

I once swore at a French woman. I didn't realise at the time I had sworn at her or accused her of being a witch! Despite the fact I cannot speak French other than to say hello and cheerio, the rude accusations were spoken in fluent French. The woman I swore at was a French lecturer on a course I attended in January 1998. She had a strong gift of discernment and had taught for several days on this subject. The teaching over, she progressed to ministry and invited response from the students, of whom I was one. I was desperate for more discernment. There were times when I thought there was something wrong with my prophetic antennae because despite my earnest desire to be one hundred percent accurate, I sometimes blundered on interpretation. This was partly because I was a young prophet in training, but not entirely. During the teaching on discernment, I felt the Holy Spirit wanted to heal me from something, but I didn't know what it was.

Just before responding to my tutor, another prophetic woman spoke a word over my life. She prayed the first chapter of Jeremiah over me, with particular emphasis on verse 5, '*Before I formed you in the womb I knew you, before you were born I set you apart; I appointed you as a prophet to the nations.*' It was as if God's fire had fallen over my entire being. The truth of those words was grafted into my spirit in that holy moment but nothing could prepare me for what would follow. I lay on the ground marvelling at God's call on my life. The wonder quickly turned to excruciating pain.

## Deliverance Ministry

I had heard about the woman Jezebel in the bible. She was a nasty piece of work in her day and apparently there was a spiritual being with the same name and nature that oppressed God's people even today. Elijah, the prophet, was God's man when confronting some of Jezebel's handiwork, which included killing many of the Lord's prophets (*1 Kings 18:4*), raising up false prophets of her own who dabbled in witchcraft (*v19*), not to mention leading the whole nation of Israel astray. Elijah called down fire from heaven and God responded with a mighty blaze (*v 36-38*) and the people turned back to God (*v39*).

Jezebel was married to king Ahab (*1 Kings 21:7*) and he was the worst king that had ever lived. The two of them perfectly fitted the bill of the 'gruesome twosome'. Basically, Jezebel killed the prophets and influenced the kings. Jezebel met her gory end when a couple of eunuchs threw her from a window. She was trampled to death (2 *Kings* 9:32-37) by young Jehu, anointed as the new king of Israel (2 *Kings* 9:6,7)

I first encountered Jezebel during a prayer assignment some six months before meeting the French teacher. God told me to fast (something, which I had never done before) and to focus my intercessory prayer on breaking the power of Jezebel. With two others, we formed a prayer chain and fasted for twenty-one days. It wasn't too difficult, because I was able to share the burden and each person only had to miss one meal a day.

On the final night of the three-week fast, we gathered to break bread together and worship God, believing for total spiritual breakthrough. The angel of the Lord appeared in the room and I fell to the floor. He had come to assist and protect us as we prayed against the Jezebel spirit. No one else in the room was able to see him, but others discerned his holy presence. I had to keep my eyes closed because of the brightness of the angel. We stopped praying eventually and the meeting concluded peacefully.

Just after God spoke his prophetic promise to me about the nations, in the next breath, I swore at the French tutor. Actually, I had absolutely no idea who was really talking, nor that it had that kind of influence on my life. I yielded immediately to the precision surgery of the Holy Spirit. There were at least five grown women praying simultaneously for me. All of them were mature teachers and several were international prayer leaders. I was in God's hands and in good hands, which was just as well really, because great strength was required to save me from strangulation.

As the women prayed, commanding Jezebel to loose its hold on my life, my hands flew to my neck and attached themselves there trying to choke the life breath out of me. I struggled to breathe and the five women had a tough time removing my hands. The demon mocked and laughed as I gasped for air. Just as the queen Jezebel was determined to annihilate the Lord's prophets in her day, the Jezebel spirit was equally determined to silence me! Eventually, I was delivered. It was a horrific experience but I am eternally grateful to Jesus for setting me free.

I was shocked I had a demon and didn't know it. I thought back to the arrows vision and the prophecy in church and wondered how I could possibly have given anything worthwhile when I still needed deliverance from Jezebel? God gave me His peace. His grace covered me in my weakness. He was pleased with my continual supplication to have a clean heart. I felt stupid when I thought of the three week fast, but the Lord ensured me it had been a fruitful time. I remembered the angel of His presence and was deeply humbled. God reminded me that my heart motivation at that time had been selfless and that was why He sent His angel. His timing is always perfect and I just had to accept that. The visions had been from Him. I asked Jesus how the Jezebel spirit had gained access to my life. He explained that it was something that had come down my family line. I had inherited it, but it was a curse rather than a blessing. The Lord removed the curse and I was free to move into the fullness of hearing His voice.

I accepted the gift of discernment right after this and it changed my world. What I had seen or known in part increased ten fold with immediate effect. For a while this was enjoyable but then the going got tough. I couldn't walk down the street without staring into people's souls with Father's absolute accuracy. It was agony to have the lives of complete strangers unfold before my eyes. As I walked the Holy Spirit talked. I passed a woman and He told me she was a battered wife; another lady would come and go, but not before He told me she was suffering from depression. In the supermarket I looked around me and saw child abusers and prostitutes. It was like having a pair of spiritual x-ray specs and it hurt like hell.

It all got too much for me and I asked the Lord to take the gift of discernment away. I guess that was quite a selfish thing to do but I was overwhelmed by the need I saw all around me. I changed my mind a while later and asked God to forgive me for rejecting His gift. He did and I started to 'know' things about people again. By this time I was more confident in Christ and understood I had to have balance in my gifting. That meant looking for the positive and not just the negative. I would sometimes share what the Lord had shown me with the person concerned. I never shared anything negative. If I discerned something awful I would take it to my prayer closet and bombard heaven for mercy. Eventually, the Lord took me beyond looking for the good in humanity to discovering the 'God' in them. I gave it a name and called it 'redemptive prophecy'. Even if I saw negative things when I prayed for someone, I turned it on its head to become a blessing. For instance, if I discerned a person suffering from rejection, I prophesied acceptance and released the spirit of son ship over them. If I discerned a cold heart I prayed the Father's abundant love and prophesied compassion. This style of praying had profound and positive effect.

Ultimately, I was healed up and trained up enough to be used by

the Lord in deliverance ministry. My first forays into demonic eviction had been personal and I knew what it felt like before, during and
after minstry – that helped! I had been flung around floorboards,
screamed at and strangled. It was pay back time!

It genuinely surprised me how many Christians were afraid of
demons. I had been fortunate enough to know first hand that demons
are powerless against Jesus word, His blood and His name. I studied
the Scriptures and copied what Jesus did. He didn't tolerate nonsense
from demons and neither would I. He called them what they were
and evicted them from the poor souls whom they were tormenting.
The gift of discernment helped me to identify the rogue demons and
the Holy Spirit living in me, set the captives free. It was glorious.

# CHAPTER 16

## COSTLY BLESSINGS

The nations were much on my heart. I had prayed faithfully for my local area, for my homeland Scotland and now I knew God was calling me to pray for the nations. I knew because He told me. I bought a huge map of the world and stuck it on my wall and started praying through the continents. I didn't have a plan, I just prayed what God showed me or told me. For two years I prayed with little of the prophetic fruit of these prayers becoming public. God stripped me of more pride as I was faithful to prophesy in the hidden place. That doesn't mean I didn't want to go to the nations I was praying for. In fact, I wanted to go so much it hurt but my family commitments made it impossible. I am ashamed to admit I even did some spiritual sulking for a while when I couldn't get my own way in this regard. God, as ever, was patient with me and accepted my heartfelt prayers of repentance when I stopped sulking!

People were occasionally critical of the fact I prayed for nations and published words via the Elijah List. People demanded to know what right I had to do such a thing. Not only was I wrestling with pride but also intimidation. At times I lost the desire to pray for the nations because the repercussions could be quite fierce. Like Elijah who had run away from the wicked queen Jezebel, even after a major spiritual breakthrough in the nation, I sometimes struggled with enemy deluge and felt isolated. God has a tender way of dealing with lonely prophets – He feeds them and gives them rest – bringing a fresh revelation of His majesty each time adverse circumstances are overcome in meekness (*1 Kings 19*).

I remember meeting a young aspiring leader in an airport lounge for a short appointment. I was unprepared for his aggressive stance. He demanded to know whom I was accountable to and if and how the words I posted were tested to be true and not counterfeit? He did not approve of Internet prophecy and then concluded his tirade by admitting he knew very little about the prophetic. There was nothing wrong with some of his questions, what was in error was his arrogant attitude. Actually, his attitude was a mere 'speck' compared to the log in my eye!

In 1999 I sent a prophecy about Canada to the Elijah List. In response I received a lovely e-mail from a lady named Pat Cocking. She thanked me for the word and asked if I would mind if she took it with her to a leaders gathering in Canada. I was delighted because the reason I posted prophetic words on the Internet was to prompt people around the world to pray.

I was humbled to receive a note from Pat. She is a gifted teacher and prophetess and carries God's heart of compassion for the church and the lost. Since '99 we have become good friends and the Lord has used Pat to help me mature as a disciple. On one occasion I sent some prophetic thoughts to several UK leaders, in response to an article I had received via the Internet. In truth, I didn't have peace in my heart after I sent the e-mail and I asked Pat to pray with me. She affirmed that she loved my intensity, but then counselled me to really ask the Lord if I had shown Wisdom in my response. I knew immediately I had been arrogant and lacked respect towards the leaders. I didn't feel I needed to rescind the prophetic response, but it was absolutely necessary to apologise for my appallingly arrogant attitude. I do so as earnestly and meekly as I know how. I learned from that gigantic blunder that prophecy must be couched in humility and wisdom or the message may be lost.

If a word is delivered in a proud way it may not be heard. Over the years, I have been confronted with a number of similar situations. Oftentimes, criticism is also expressed on the issue of gender, with the disapproval of women in leadership roles being stated or implied. I've learned that the best response is humility, although this response is often the most difficult to attain. I gently informed the aspiring young leader that I did have accountability and coached him in testing a prophetic word:

· *Does the prophecy line up with the nature and character of God? If a prophecy lacks mercy it is not from the Lord. If a prophecy displays rejection or a critical attitude it may be that person giving the prophecy needs some healing in one or more of these areas.*

· *Does the prophecy line up with Scripture? It doesn't have to be Scripture but a true word from the Lord will not be in contradiction to the Bible. God never compromises His own holiness.*

· *Is there a witness (the feel 'right' factor in God) in your spirit to the Spirit of the prophecy? If not, it may not be from the Lord*

· *Does the prophet/prophecy display the humility of Christ?*

· *Is there fruit in the prophet's life that honours Father?*

# The Normal, The Deep and The Crazy

*These bullet points were simple guidelines I had learned as I went along. The best advice is that of The Word itself,*

*'Do not put out the Spirit's fire; do not treat prophecies with contempt. Test everything. Hold on to the good. Avoid every kind of evil.'*
                                                              1 Thessalonians 5:19-22

When I was on an intensive learning curve about prophecy I mistakenly thought prayer could take a lower profile. Pride almost crept into my prayer closet but after a short wrestle, the Lord ensured I understood that prayer and prophecy are inseparable.

During this season I learned more about the authority of Christ over nations. They belong to Him – they are his inheritance (*Psalms 2:8*). There is nowhere on earth that we can set our feet that Father has not already given to Jesus. I prayed from this position of security. It was easy to pray God's will for a nation when I truly believed they were his. My faith soared and the prophetic anointing deepened and matured. I asked for more faith and received it.

*'We each have different gifts according to the grace given us. If a man's gift is prophesying, let him use it in proportion to his faith.' Romans 12:6*

## March for Jesus

In the summer of 1997 I had a vision of children worshipping Jesus and marching through the glen in our village. I was inspired to pray about this and in answer to my entreaty the Lord set my feet on an unexpected path.

Somewhere, somehow, I heard about Graham Kendrick and the March for Jesus. I wondered if the Lord was trying to speak to me about hosting a March for Jesus in West Kilbride. I didn't think I had the know-how or the courage to organise such an event. I laid a fleece before the Lord in prayer – I asked Him to confirm if this was His will by granting me favour with the three local church leaders. One by one, I made appointments to see each man and, one by one, they agreed to back the venture. Now I'd done it, or rather the Holy Spirit had!

I contacted Jim Woodrow the Scottish MFJ organiser and told him about the vision, about the pastoral backing and asked him for help. Jim gave me brilliant advice from contacting police to obtain permission to march, to planning the route, taking out public liability insurance, arranging the music and the thousand other things that needed to be in place for the march to be a success.

I witnessed my first multiplication miracle when I was preparing information packs to send out about the march. I needed 1800 leaflets and I only had 1000. It was all we could afford at the time. I put what I had on the table and prayed and asked Jesus to make it enough. I started folding, with Mark giving a hand. After a while Mark got bored and left. He came back later and was surprised to find I was still sealing envelopes. We counted the leaflets – we had 1800. To say we were gob smacked is an understatement. Mark thought I had cheated or had made the whole thing up but the truth was I started with one thousand leaflets and ended with eighteen hundred. Man's extremity is God's opportunity!

There were just four weeks to go before the big day. I was excited but also extremely tired and frustrated at the lack of practical support I had received despite initial offers of help they simply never materialised. During this season I had been praying for a Jewish lady. She was the mother of a man I met earlier in January, when I had enrolled on a weeklong series of seminars on God's heart for the Jewish people..

### Jesus - King of the Jews

Prior to meeting my mentor Tony, I had been fairly indifferent towards the Jewish people. I had no particular prejudice against Jews, but neither did I hold them with any deep affection in my heart. The politics of the Middle East intimidated me, and this, significantly, contributed to my position of ignorance. For a myriad of reasons, I had never taken the time to discover God's heart for the Jewish people. It seems a rather absurd thing to say, but somehow I had never really noticed them when I read the Bible! I had neither grasped nor seen the beautiful love affair between Yahweh and the Israelites, nor had I understood that it was of deep significance to me personally and also to the future of worldwide revival.

*'Again I ask: did they stumble so as to fall beyond recovery? Not al all! Rather, because of their transgression, salvation has come to the Gentiles to make Israel envious. But if their transgression means riches for the world, and their loss means riches for the Gentiles, how much greater riches will their fullness bring.' Romans 11:11, 12*

The teaching of the Messianic believer radically challenged me. Eliyahu was a born again Jew who was filled with the Holy Spirit. He spent a week sharing with us on the Father's heart for Israel - the people and the land. I experienced intense emotional and spiritual 'highs and lows' throughout this time.

On the last day of the week I was invited to lead a prayer time for one hour. I had been given plenty of notice for the assignment and was fully prepared despite the fact I had never led a prayer concert before. On the Friday morning the Holy Spirit spoke to me and asked if I would lay down what I had prepared and use the time to pray for the Jewish people instead.

We broke for lunch and I went off to pray trying not to have a blind blue fit. I asked the Lord for inspiration because I had no clue how to pray for Israel. I was drawn to a dressmaker's shop where I purchased some yellow material. I hurriedly cut it into squares and carried it in to the classroom with me. I explained to the group of around thirty people that God had asked me to pray for the Jews, but I wasn't sure how to do that. I shared my emotional journey of how Jesus had moved me from a personal position of indifference, through hostility and sibling jealousy, to repentance and finally receiving an incredible heaven-sent love for my 'elder brother'. At the start of the week I didn't even know Jesus proper name was Yeshua but now I rejoiced in the fact He was, and is, the King of the Jews. I invited the students to come and take a piece of yellow cloth and place it on their hearts and ask Father for His heart for the Jews. I ensured everyone knew it was not a compulsory exercise and asked people to come forward only if they were prompted by the Lord. I have never before or since seen such an instantaneous spiritual explosion in a room.

People almost ran to the front of the room to take a piece of cloth. The depth of response was beyond words. Students wept violently as God grafted His love for the Jews into our hearts. We just melted. Simultaneously, several students started screaming and manifesting demonic behaviour at the back of the classroom. They had anti Semitic influences in their lives and the power of God was so strongly present that it broke their spiritual bondage.

### Everlasting love

I studied the Scriptures and the Holy Spirit helped me to understand that the Lord loves Israel with an everlasting love and that the gentile church has an important role to play in praying for the Jewish people. I learned that God's principle is 'the Jew first'.

*"I am not ashamed of the gospel, because it is the power of God for the salvation of everyone who believes: first for the Jew, then for the Gentile"*
*Romans 1:16*

To demonstrate His faithfulness in the principle of 'the Jew first', the Lord asked me to pray for Eliyahu's mother. She was elderly and not in good health and she didn't believe Jesus was her Messiah. The prayer carried a condition of trust – I was to stop praying for my own mum and have confidence in the Lord to save them both. I did what the Lord asked me.

### Goodbye Mum

Just four weeks before the March for Jesus an emotional bomb detonated in my heart, from which it took me a long time to recover. We received a late night telephone call to say that my mum had suffered a massive heart attack. I jumped into the car and cried out to God, "Can I pray for my mum?" He gave me permission to pray for my mum, instructing me to lay hands on her and believe that He would heal her heart.

When I arrived at mum's place my sister was already present and the doctor looked extremely concerned. Mum's face was grey and her breathing laboured as she lay on her bed clutching a Bible I asked with tenderness, "Mum, can I pray for you"? She answered "yes", and I got on to the bed, laid hands on her and with every ounce of faith in me, I prayed to Jesus and asked Him to heal her heart. I immediately felt power go out from me, and I knew the Lord had healed her – my assumption was that it was physical.

Mum was rushed to hospital and for the next two days she battled for her life. After mum's heart rate had stabilised, I was able to visit her. She smiled weakly at me and was able to whisper "Catherine, there are angels in this room. You prayed for me, I felt something". With tears running down my face, I agreed with mum about the angels and that Jesus was the Healer and had healed her heart. Mum smiled and nodded an acceptance that went far deeper than the incline of her head. God's glory was tangible. During those final hours friends and saints from around the world joined us in a prayer vigil for mum. The prayers I had sown for Eliyahu's mum, were returned one hundred fold. The Wisdom for me had been in obeying God.

I recall walking through the hospital late on the first night of mum's admission. The corridor was dark and deserted. I was emotionally drained. Suddenly, a beautiful man appeared from nowhere. He approached me and said "Peace be with you. Do not be afraid. Please don't cry – your mother is in God's hands". Smiling, he walked away, literally vanishing into thin air. Several hours later I realised the Lord had sent an angel to minister to me in my brokenness.

Two days later, mum passed away into the arms of Jesus. In my grief I decided to ask the Lord to resurrect mum, and went along with two close friends to pray for her. We stood in front of my mother's casket in a small funeral parlour, with extremely thin partition walls and began to call on God for His resurrection power! After a few moments, I felt a release from the Lord to stop praying.

At that precise moment, a joy I have never experienced before or since welled up in me and I began to praise God at the top of my lungs. It was as though I was being permitted to touch a tiny fragment of the joy my dear mother was experiencing at that very moment in heaven. I knew that I had gained an incredible spiritual victory in that moment. Just like Leah (Genesis 29) I had learned to praise God despite my circumstances. The time was sealed by a vision of my mum dancing before Jesus. It was awesome.

The funeral parlour director had an incredulous expression on his face when we exited the room! I pray that one day someone will walk out of that room with resurrection glory written all over them and that many will be saved through their witness! On returning home I will forever remember my husband's eyes of faith as he looked out of our kitchen window, expecting four people to exit the car and not just three.

So it was and is a profound work of the Holy Spirit as he reveals Father's heart for the Jewish people to me. I have rediscovered the Word of God, and I am humbly seeking to understand the culture of Jewish people. I hold them with intense affection in my heart. I pray that my mother is smiling on me from heaven as I share these words, that are also a testimony to her love for me and Christ's love for us all – Jew and Gentile alike.

### Israel the beloved – a vision

*'On this mountain He will destroy the shroud that enfolds all peoples, the sheet that covers all nations; He will swallow up death forever. The Sovereign Lord will wipe away the tears from all faces; He will remove the disgrace of His people from all the earth, the Lord has spoken.' Isaiah 25:7-8*

I found myself looking down on the earth, from a heavenly perspective. I saw the Lord lift a shroud (a large white veil) from the land of Israel, and it seemed as though a veil was lifted from the whole earth. The Lord spoke these words: "Once more My people will know their Beloved, and that they are My beloved. No more shall their eyes be blind nor their hearts remain hard towards My eternal love. Now the time has come for the immutable promises of the Father to be revealed in all the earth, and for the prisoners to be released and the captives to be set free." Let those who have an ear to hear listen to what the Spirit says."

The symbolism of the veil being removed represents salvation for Israel, just as the Bible has promised.

*'In that day they will say, "Surely this is our God; we trusted in Him and He saved us. This is the Lord we trusted Him; Let us rejoice and be glad in His salvation.' Isaiah 25:9*

The shroud being lifted by the Saviour indicated the veil being removed from the hearts and minds of the children of Israel, to permit them to embrace their Saviour Yeshua - this will bring great blessings to the earth.

*'God gave them a spirit of stupor, eyes so that they could not see and ears that they could not hear," Again I ask: Did they stumble so as to fall beyond recovery? Not at all! Rather because of their transgression, salvation has come to the Gentiles to make Israel envious. But if their transgression means riches for the world, and their loss means riches for the Gentiles, how much greater riches will their fullness bring.' Romans 11:8, Romans 11:11-12*

The vision speaks of the promised redemption of the children of Israel and their reconciliation with Father God.

*"For I will take you out of the nations; I will gather you from all the countries and bring you back into your own land. I will sprinkle clean water on you, and you will be clean; I will cleanse you from all your impurities and from all your idols. I will give you a new heart and put a new spirit in you; I will remove from you your heart of stone and give you a heart of flesh. And I will put My Spirit in you and move you to follow my decrees and be careful to keep my laws. You will live in the land I gave your forefathers; you will be my people, and I will be your God." Exodus 36:24-28*

The salvation of the children of Israel is a gem of indescribable beauty in the Lord's eyes

*'The Lord their God will save them on that day as the flock of His people. They will sparkle in His land like jewels in a crown. How attractive and beautiful they will be!' Zechariah 9:16*

### God is not prejudiced

One thing I know for sure - God is not prejudiced. The Bible affirms this in *Galatians 3:26-28*. The Jewish people are His firstborn son, but that does not mean the Lord loves any other nation of people in a lesser way and this includes those who are currently enslaved to the religion of Islam. When God says His desire is that none should perish and all should come to repentance (*2 Peter 3:9*) that is exactly what He means. With this in mind, some years after my mother's death, I prayed for Iraq. This vision is the fruit of those prayers. In the current climate of war, it is powerful to pray in the opposite spirit of love and hope.

### A vision of hope for Iraq

*'Why are you downcast, O my soul? Why so disturbed within me? Put your hope in God, for I will yet praise him, my Saviour and my God.' Psalms 42:5*

In the Spirit, I saw a beautiful firework display over Iraq. The fireworks were of the most eye-catching colours. It was vibrant display of light, sound and colour. I asked the Lord, 'what are they'? He replied,

*'Child, these are cluster bursts of prayer inspired by the Holy Spirit. Each time the prayers of my people explode over Iraq, seeds of hope are being deposited in the hearts of the people and in the land. Tell my children that I desire they pray like Joshua and Caleb for they had a different spirit - they prayed with eyes of faith and with a vision for victory. My desire is that none should perish and that all should come to repentance. My children, do not focus on the giants, but rather on the fruit of the accomplishment of Calvary. In the Spirit, prayer walk the land, for there is no place that you can place your feet that My Father has not already given to me as my inheritance. In the Spirit, possess the land; make declaration over Iraq that it belongs to My Father and Me. Boldly proclaim My kingdom come. Do not be not afraid, neither be discouraged. Pray with belief, not unbelief in your hearts. Trust in Me. See with eyes of faith and align yourselves with My Word, for therein lies my will.*

*Pray for my church in Iraq, that every believer will be strengthened with new hope. Say 'no' to intimidation, say 'no' to exaggeration and say 'no' to isolation; be clothed in faith and holy boldness, proclaim My truth, and seek unity in the Spirit with all of your hearts.*

*I desire to orchestrate a global concert of prayer. I Am is your conductor. There are millions of needs in prayer and millions are needed to pray. It takes many notes to produce a harmony, and I will likewise use the diversity amongst my people to bring harmony to their prayers and to release a prayer concert of hope that will deliver the nations. My children, those of you who dance - dance for the deliverance of a nation. Those of you whom I have gifted as artists, allow me to creatively inspire the work of your hands to be freedom fighters of the Kingdom. Those of you who sing, permit Me to bring songs of deliverance through you. Wave a banner and make proclamation of My Mercy. You are ALL My intercessors, yet precious children, you must realise the intercession is by My Spirit. Yield and surrender to His ways.'*

I am struck by the profound simplicity of this word. What impacts me is the beauty of hope for a nation (Iraq) through Jesus Christ. Instead of cluster bombs that tear the very lifeblood from a nation, the Lord wants to release cluster explosions of glory - prayers filled with hope and healing, releasing His light into the darkness of Islam! God will direct our prayers, because He desires a global prayer concert. That means we will pray in agreement with the Father. It also means that our prayers may not necessarily all sound or look the same. We must exercise Godly wisdom and not judge one another's petitions.

The Lord is releasing us to creatively intercede for the nations. He is looking for those who will sing, dance, scribe, paint, sculpt, worship and pray His kingdom come. Get out your maps and lay hands on Iraq and boldly declare the land and the people are the inheritance of Christ!

Praying with a vision for victory does not mean we have to pray from a political view point and neither does it mean we have to take a particular military stance. To pray with a vision of victory, is to pray with our eyes fixed on Jesus and the victory of Calvary - the price He paid for all mankind.

### A sacrifice of praise

Life without mum was painful. Despite our differences, I loved her deeply and missed her zany sense of humour and warmth. In mourning her loss, the last thing I felt like doing was marching round my hometown and singing songs of celebration, but you know what? That is precisely what I did. Up until a few days before the March for Jesus, hardly anyone had responded to the 1800 fliers we had sent out and I wondered if we should cancel. Stephen said, 'precious, if we have to march around the village just the five of us and a CD player that's what we will do, but whatever happens we are going ahead with this march.' It was settled.

The day arrived and the sun shone gloriously. At the last minute, several kind people came forward to help. At the final count I think we had a few hundred marchers. There were some problems with the sound system but we sang anyway. We hired a Christian clown who made extraordinary creations with balloons, we sported brightly coloured hats and streamers and beautiful banners. Our focus for the march was the persecuted church and the dramas poignantly brought home the message of sacrificial love. We were able to raise a large sum of money as a donation for the suffering church. I was nowhere up front on the day; other people led the prayer sections. Despite having invested months of my life and pouring myself into the project, God gave me the reward of allowing others to shine. I put on my best smile and did it for Jesus and thought how proud my mum would be looking down on me from heaven.

### Promotion!

Jim at March for Jesus, Scotland was so impressed with my hard work and dedication; he invited me to be part of the organising group for a national prayer and worship event, backed by MFJ. I was thrilled and terrified all over again. Here was the principle of being faithful with little in action once more. It seemed God was promoting me.

I attended the first committee meeting in September '98 and was over awed by the wealth of amazing leaders in the room. This aside, I was the only woman! Afterwards, I told Jim privately that I didn't think I was qualified for helping out on such a grand event. He smiled at me and said 'Catherine, I love your heart. I want to you to be our prayer co-ordinator.' I took up the challenge with my usual gusto and threw myself into the role. I sought the Lord for a strategy and He inspired me with ideas for three national prayer events, all of which took place within eighteen months.

### Baby number four

I was happy doing things for Jesus. I liked my routine and I didn't want it to be disturbed thank you very much! God had other ideas and in November of 1998 I discovered that baby number four was on the way. We couldn't believe it. We thought our family was complete and had given away all our baby things. In truth, I didn't relish the thought of more sleepless nights and dirty nappies!

I wondered if I would have to lay everything down. In addition to my duties with MFJ, I also enjoyed helping out in our church as a Sunday school teacher, as well as spending time hanging out with the street kids who came to the drop in centre on Friday nights. To top it all, I launched my own small business and was working from home making wedding favours! I found this rewarding and exhausting and didn't think I would have the energy to be pregnant, look after my other three children and my husband, keep house and do all of the above.

I was wrong. The Holy Spirit gave me supernatural strength and resourced me for the next nine months. I worked like a dog and gave everything I could to prepare for the new baby, serve my family and continue in ministry. The only thing I gave up was my business. During this period the foundations were laid for a children's prayer tour of Scotland and a three-day women's prayer conference in Edinburgh. As if that wasn't enough I also embarked on organising a mission trip for two Argentine pastors to Scotland!

## Bob, Paul and Nita

Towards the end of 1998 Tony, my accountability buddy, had to move on due to work commitments. I completely understood his reasons it left a void in terms of my support.

In February 1999 the Lord linked me with some key people moving in prophetic things in the USA through an interesting chain of events. I had sent a personal prophecy to Misty, an assistant of the Elijah List. She mistakenly sent a thank you note for this word to one of these men and he didn't understand why he had received the note so he asked Misty to send him a copy of the word. Misty sent this to these two men whose interest was stirred. In the words of one of the guys, 'the fire of God is all over it'. In fact, a sermon had been preached some time previously, using almost identical language to my own.

Misty then wrote to me and explained what had been going on. She apologised for any confusion. There was no apology necessary! I was delighted because I had prayed about being in contact with these men, but had no e-mail address. Something Paul Keith said in those early communications has stuck with me to this day. When I asked if they would be willing to weigh the prophecies I was receiving, I assumed they would be too busy. The reply came, 'if we are too busy to help you, then indeed, we are too busy'. It inspired me to model this principle in my own life and give generously of myself and my time to young men and women who are seriously seeking the 'more' of Jesus.

Paul is a gifted writer and prophetic teacher. He assisted me in my early writing endeavours. He, his wife Wanda, Bob Jones and Nita Johnson brought great encouragement to my life and gifting.

## Samuel the bullet

My health was excellent throughout the pregnancy but I was a little bit anxious about the birthing process, after my traumatic experience when Rebecca was born. The doctor's informed me I would be given a short trial of labour but I would probably have to have another c-section for a safe delivery. I did not want this to happen and Stephen and I prayed for God's intervention. My labour pains started at home and as I crawled around on all fours breathing through my contractions, I asked God to release the youth of Scotland and the nations. I know this sounds strange and peculiar, but it was in line with so much the Lord had been communicating to me. As well as the physical labour pains I experienced enormous spiritual travail. It was a crazy scenario. We left for the hospital and arrived just thirty minutes before our new baby was born. God sent Samuel the bullet! He whooshed into the world after three enormous pushes and we were thrilled to have another son.

The sacrificial aspect of praise continued to deepen. I had a new-born baby, a three year old, a five year old and a ten year old. I loved them and my husband outrageously, but in spite of this, I loved Jesus more. I wanted to fast, but couldn't, because I was breast-feeding Samuel. God gave me the grace to fast from sleep, so instead of going back to bed between the 2.00 a.m. and 6.00 a.m. feeds I stayed awake and spent the time with my Lord. I did this for about six weeks. These were the best of times. His presence was thick and exquisite. My heart was fascinated with the beauty of Jesus. During the day I was sometimes exhausted to the point of collapse, but I didn't want to stop. I took naps instead.

From this season an absolute torrent of words for the nations was released. I had never experienced such a non-stop prophetic flow as during this time. India, Africa, Australia, America and Europe - it just kept on coming, nation by nation.

### The Holy Spirit fireball

The mission trip I had organised for the two Argentine pastors was upon us. The six of us piled into the car and headed for Arbroath to the meetings. Whilst I was there, I had a new experience of the divine person of the Holy Spirit. I actually saw him as a fireball! The Argentine pastor was walking towards me praying in tongues. As he lifted his hands towards me a massive ball of fire was released in the Spirit and it catapulted across the room and hit me square in the heart. From that day to this, the Holy Spirit has been more real than he ever was.

I've always tried to be honest with my children and sharing my spiritual experiences with them is something I have endeavoured to do. I haven't always been successful but I have tried. Along the way, the Lord has blessed and bypassed my stutters. When Rebecca was four years old she came to me and asked, 'How can Jesus be in heaven and be in my heart mummy?' (We had been talking a lot about the Cross, the Resurrection, and the Holy Spirit). I told her Jesus sends the Holy Spirit into our hearts. She reflected quietly then responded, 'my heart is empty mummy.'

I marvelled in that moment at this tiny scrap of humanity laying hold of the most important truth of all – she was empty without Christ and only the Holy Spirit could fill the aching void in her heart.

Many people live their whole lives without ever discovering this Truth. Rebecca proceeded to get under our kitchen table and began to pray. I got under the table too and joined her. She invited Jesus to be her Lord and Saviour, repenting for her sin and then we prayed for the Holy Spirit to come and fill her empty heart. I anointed Rebecca with oil and she did the same to me.

## Women of courage

In February of 2000, the first of the national prayer events from '98 came into being. I had never attended a prayer conference let alone organise one, however the Lord helped me every step of the way. From choosing the hotel, to arranging speakers, flowers, a bookstall, sound equipment, recording of tapes, worship leaders and formalising the prayer strategy God was faithful! He even gave me a wonderful mentor in the shape of my friend Jean Black.

I had a vision in my heart to see an army raised for God's glory. I felt afraid and un-knowledgeable but I knew God wouldn't let me down. Faith doesn't mean you don't sometimes feel afraid – it's about pushing past the fear and pursuing God's unique call on your life.

At this time I was reading a book entitled, 'Women on the Front Lines' by Michal Ann Goll. It was full of stories about women of faith, who gave their lives as martyrs for Jesus. Joan of Arc was one such woman. She had fascinated me since I was a small child and reading of her heroic deeds inspired me. By the age of seventeen she was leading men on the battlefields of France, fighting for her country and her king. She said, 'I have a vision from God,' He has called me to raise an army for our nation and for Him.' On July 17, 1429 Charles VII was crowned king of France with Joan standing as a witness, after she had led French troops to defeat the English along the Loire River, and capturing the city of Troyes along the way.

Despite her courage she was betrayed and handed over to the English authorities, who falsely accused her of being a witch and a heretic. She was condemned to her death. At just nineteen was burnt at the stake for her love of Christ. She called out for a cross and poured out words of forgiveness and mercy against those who had treated her so unjustly. It's said her heart would not burn – it was pure and consumed already with the fire of holy passion for Jesus. Her executioner was filled with remorse and recognised the holiness of the teenager who had been slain. Twenty-five years after she died a martyr Joan's case was re-opened and she was cleared of all accusations and considered a French national heroine. The Catholic Church made her a saint in 1920.

These kinds of true stories stirred and motivated me to press in for all God had planned for my life. I longed to bring Him glory. Joan didn't know how to read or write and had no experience of war when she entered her first battle. She simply trusted the Voice of God and knew her Father would guide and counsel her no matter what. With this in mind, I was determined not to give up!

Just a few days before the conference I was busy with last minute preparations. Alarmingly, only a handful of people had registered to attend and we needed around £2000 to break even. I had a promise of faith in my heart from Jesus that I was to persevere and believe that He would send the women and cover the expenses. Stephen and I and our four kids left for Edinburgh on the intrepid wings of faith. I was thrilled and relieved when over one hundred and fifty women turned up on the first day! I was a no-body from nowhere and they came not for me but because God had called them. God opened up the heavenly bank accounts too, and by day three of the conference we were in the black! I discovered that God is no man's debtor.

I shared with the women that only seven years before I had been afraid to pray out loud. I encouraged them to press in for all that God had for them because if He could transform me, He could change anyone. It was my first public preach and I was so nervous that unfortunately I had diarrhoea for the entire three days of the conference. On listening to the tapes I realised I had a few idiosyncrasies including saying 'em' quite a bit. My speaking skills definitely needed a little polish. On the final day of the conference I carried an old rugged cross I had constructed from driftwood collected from the beach, to the top of Edinburgh Castle. There, with around fifty other women, we prayed and worshipped to bagpipe music!

Just before the conference, I had a vision of women being lifted into the heavens. Angels received the women, and eventually each lady was granted a personal appearance with the Lord. Despite the fact that there were countless women each had an intimate encounter with Christ. He cradled each woman's face in His hands and spoke, *"Well done, good and faithful servant"*, and on each cheek he planted a tender kiss. The favour of God was spoken over everyone.

The angels gave out weaponry and each woman was equipped for battle. The weapons spoke of the faithfulness of God's character. The women received fresh revelation of the Grace, mercy and unchanging nature of God; the banner of His Righteousness over them was without blemish. They were then despatched to the north, the south, the east and the west and were equipped to wage war.

*"Women of God arise. Women of weeping arise. Women of courage and*

*women of destiny come forth from thy hiding places, see thy hiding place is now in My Shekinah. Your labours of love have not been hidden from My sight. It is time to come out of your prayer closets and to link up and to link arms across this land. Region to region, My Spirit shall bring about divine connections and Holy alliances. Many of you have felt as though My Spirit and My Presence have departed from Your land, but see the season of bareness has come to an end and the wilderness shall come forth from desolation into fruitfulness. The spirit of Hannah shall release Samuel to the nations. The spirit of Miriam shall bring forth the new sound for revival. The spirit of Elizabeth shall birth many apostolic sons and daughters who will prepare a people for the Lord, and the spirit of Mary shall release faith and humble obedience as My Spirit overshadows my children, to bring forth apostolic anointing.*

*I have not departed from you; I stepped back only in order that you might press in for more of Me. See, the wilderness shall bloom and you shall go forth a mighty army in My Name. Women of courage arise; see your Saviour goes before you and the hosts of heaven war on your behalf. Take courage, humble yourself under My mighty hand and press forward in faith for your destinies.*

### Footnote

We enter the battle from a place of rest, and there is no more beautiful resting place than in His loving embrace. The Lord is teaching His church of the beauty of bridal intercession – worship and warfare through purity, passion and intimacy. The love of Christ poured out on His Bride and the expression of His love through her will win the nations and wreak havoc on the kingdom of darkness. Hallelujah!

# CHAPTER 17

## THE CHILDREN

Jesus loves children and I do too. It has been a learning experience raising four of my own children. The Lord has taught me lessons about recognising, listening and responding to His voice expressed through children and young people. I often made mistakes, but I think I'm beginning to get the hang of it now!

Once in church, Rebecca turned to me and said, 'we are all God's family.' I laughed out loud and agreed. She looked at me with great seriousness, and said it again, 'no mummy you don't understand – we are all God's family.' She said it loudly and with a quiet confidence. I realised then that God was speaking and affirming that from the youngest to the eldest in church we each have a legitimate place of belonging in his family. God sees us all as children – not fathers, mothers, and grandparents – just children. That set me thinking. Did I really believe that God could use a tiny child as effectively as an adult? Did I truly accept that the Holy Spirit would or could use a child to minister? At this point, I did not. I thought children were cute, cuddly and drew nice pictures. It didn't occur to me that they could be anointed by the Holy Spirit and used for miracles. I thank God that he showed me my error and changed my mind.

### Children can see and hear God

Rebecca had a visit from Jesus when she was just two and a half years old. We were going through a traumatic time as a family and on one particular day I was weeping at the kitchen table. She came to me, held me and said, 'don't cry mummy, it's ok, Jesus is here.' She pointed to the corner of the room. 'Can't you see Him mummy'? I couldn't see Jesus that day but God ministered to my broken heart through my little girl and the reality of His touch on her life. Rebecca still remembers the day Jesus came to speak with her. She often asks me when will He come and talk to her again?

Another time Rebecca came to me and said she had heard God say her name. I almost dismissed this but the Holy Spirit prompted me to listen carefully to her. 'What do you mean?' I responded. 'Mummy I asked Jesus could I at least hear Him say my name once. He said it. He just said 'Rebecca''. Children and young people hear God's voice – of that there is now no doubt in my mind.

### Worshipping Warriors

Three years ago, I took a small group of young girls out on street mission in the village where we live. It was the evening of Halloween and we wanted to worship Jesus and bring His light into the darkness. Our resources were limited to passion filled hearts, a small CD player and a six-foot fire banner! With some trepidation, we took our place on a street corner and began to worship the Lord with all our hearts. The music was barely audible, but we sang as loudly as we could.

The streets were choc a bloc with children and young people dressed as witches, warlocks and other ghouls. The reaction to the worship was immediate and violent. A group of youths gathered across the road from us and began to pelt apples at our tiny troupe of five. I prayed in the name of Jesus and cancelled the enemy's assignment to bring us harm, releasing blessings on the teenage boys who were swearing and shouting at us. The youths continued to throw the apples, which exploded all around us, but miraculously not one of them hit the intended targets – us!

Rebecca is a quiet girl, with huge blue eyes and a deep love for Christ. She rarely takes the lead and at four years old, I was concerned that if an apple hit her, she might be knocked off balance and hurt. Not so Rebecca! My little girl lifted the fire flag and took up a position at the head of our party. She marched out from our stationary point onto the streets, holding the six-foot fire flag as high as she could. The wind blew, and the painted silk and the red, orange and gold of the flag brandished the skyline with glory. The glory of a child's faith.

I willingly followed my daughter and each of our group fell in line behind her. The anointing of God was so powerfully upon her that the apples immediately stopped flying at us, and she led us up the streets, silently and in obedience to Christ her Captain. I was reminded of Isaiah's words, "a little child shall lead them". How humbled I was by her holy boldness; my spiritual eyes were further opened to the power of children and young people worshipping Jesus Christ, their Lord and Saviour (*Psalms 8:2*).

In Glasgow city, George Square there is a magnificent statue of a lion, which stands some eight feet tall. Whilst taking part in a prayer and praise event there, my young son Daniel climbed on top of the lion and held on to its mane. He smiled ecstatically at me and waved excitedly from his vantage point, whilst his big brother Mark, along with many other young people, took part in a lively dance to the tune of "The River of God sets our Feet A-Dancing". My heart swelled with love for them both, and my earnest prayer was "Oh Father, let them dare to go higher into your purposes on the wings of faith than we have every dreamed". What safer place could there be to do so, than holding tightly to the Lion of the tribe of Judah!

Once I was telling Mark about the story of Lucifer and his fall from heaven *(Ezekiel 28:12-17)*. I told him all about the guardian cherub who rose up in pride and was cast out of heaven *(Isaiah 14:11-15)*. Mark looked pensive for a moment then said, 'Mum, do you think that made God sad?' I had never thought about it like that, but it made me stop and consider the pain Father must have felt at being rejected by one He created in love. Young people have a way of asking questions that turns your head around. They have keen spiritual insight if we can overcome our pride as adults to even begin to notice.

### Gold and glory

For the first week of Samuel's life, his face was covered in gold dust. We would wipe it off and then go back a while later to admire our new family addition only to discover there was more in its place. God has used Samuel in ministry since he has been a tiny wee boy. At the tender age of two he watched with me as the September 11 disaster unfolded on the CNN news bulletins. He asked me why I was crying and I explained (using ridiculously adult words) that many innocent people had died and it was very sad. He looked at me and said three words before walking away, 'They need Jesus.' If I hadn't heard them myself I might not have believed it. But those were God's words spoken through my small son. He was right.

A friend came to our home and was in need of prayer and encouragement. We talked for over an hour and I was just about to pray for her. Samuel walked into the kitchen, pulled a stool over to the worktop and climbed on to the surface. He picked a CD, opened the CD player and put it in. I was just about to tell him to mind his own business, when the Holy Spirit said, *'No Catherine, you mind your own business. Let him be.'* Samuel chose a track on the CD and pressed the play button. The track was entitled 'Lord, make me a miracle too' and was sung by a child. The anointing fell like a mighty river in the room and my friend received God's ministry through a two year old.

### Children and young people are God's ministers

I now believe with all of my heart that the Lord can and does use children and young people for His glory. Their ability to be obedient, and do what Jesus asks of them, when and how He asks them to do it, makes them pliable living clay in the Master Potter's hands. We have much to learn from their radical obedience and innocent belief in God being just who He says He is. God had annihilated my ridiculous presumption that the Holy Spirit might minister in some lesser way through young people by sometimes bypassing me and choosing to minister through my own children instead. I'm grateful He allowed me to be humbled in this way. I can see more clearly because of it.

As we pray for God's kingdom to come on earth as it is in heaven, let our prayers also be lifted on behalf of the children and youth of the nations, who are mighty ambassadors for Christ. It is time for them to take their place in God's End Time Army!

### Take the land

During April 2000, I had the privilege of partnering with a group of children and young people in a praise and prayer tour of Scotland. The aim of the tour was to release young people to spearhead Holy Spirit-led meetings, which were held all around Scotland over a ten-day period. The organising group of adults worked with the children, supporting and serving them to fulfil the vision. We brought together a group of young people from across the nation to form the tour team. The youngest child was our daughter Rebecca, then aged four and the eldest was seventeen. We also had several young adults age 18-25 as core team members.

As part of the line-up we were delighted to welcome a group of praying young people from Australia, who were led by Jane Mackie, co-ordinator of the Children's Prayer Network. I am indebted to Graeme Young, Harry Sprange, Jane Crouch, Lynn Howson and Alan Wigglesworth for their hard work and dedication to the vision.

The children were awesome and although the trip was not always plain sailing it was powerful in its pioneering spirit, breaking new ground and uprooting some of the misconceptions adults hold regarding children and young people in ministry. I taught the children how to prophesy; others coached them in leading small groups. One woman became a Christian in a meeting in Culloden without anyone witnessing to her or praying with her. We just worshipped and prayed and God did the saving.

Throughout the 'take the land' prayer tour, we were continually challenged to 'walk the walk' and not just 'talk the talk'. It wasn't easy to get the balance right between teaching, coaching, delegating responsibility, resourcing, blessing and releasing the young people but we did our best to get it right. There were some tears and tantrums along the way, as well as a few misunderstandings between adults and young people, but we ended the tour on a positive reconciliatory note.

### Prayer for Australia – extract from a vision

I was shown Ayers Rock (Uluru) resplendent in its rugged beauty, with many people gathered around and on the mountain. There was a holy silence and an awe of God that came over the people as they waited in hushed and expectant faith. It was the moment before birth - a stilling. Suddenly, the Glory of the Lord broke forth on Ayers Rock, and like a volcano ribbons of exquisite satin unfurled from the top of the mountain and cascaded all the way down to its base and beyond. The colours of the satin were distinctly separate from one another and flowed like a river. They were purple, red, azure blue, gold and white. The satin ribbons were held high, being carried on the arms of young people and children. The children ran down the mountain full of the joy of the Lord. They were carrying the Lord's banner and I noticed that Jehovah Nissi was inscribed on each of the coloured satins.

The satin flowed out from the Glory of God and speaks of the restoration in Australia of the royal priesthood (purple), prophetic mantle (blue), righteousness of Christ (white), sovereignty of God (gold) and the sanctification of the Blood of Christ (red) as it flows as a river of life from Ayers Rock.

I was shown Aboriginal and white adults running together down the mountain. The Aboriginals and whites then lay down together to form a human footpath. The children who had previously carried the Lord's banner joined the human footpath and became the supporting pillars, still holding high the magnificent banners of Truth. How precious to see Aboriginal men and white men in the perfect bond of peace and unity in the Spirit. The children also formed an integral part of the bridge, becoming the pillars of truth that supported the bridge. The banner over the whole bridge was the name of the Lord - Almighty God. I gazed in wonder as the Lord's Throne descended majestically from heaven and was placed on Ayer's Rock.

### Prophecy

*"I am going to establish My Throne on this mountain,* says the Lord. *"I will hear your prayers for open heaven in this place and you will see my angels coming up and going down. Just as in Korea I established Prayer Mountain, so shall I call forth Ayers Rock as a Prayer Mountain in Australia. Indeed, watch for my prayer mountains to be established in all the earth. Many shall come to this place on a holy pilgrimage to enter into My Presence. My beloved Australia this is the day of your Redemption, and I will answer your humble prayers for you have moved the Father to deep compassion for this land and for its people. I am opening up deep wells of refreshing to bring this barren desert into bloom. I am sending forth my children to the ends of the earth, equipped to carry My Banner.*

*I am restoring My Bride and releasing a new anointing of sanctification to the royal priesthood. You will move in the unity and the bond of peace of My Spirit. Yield your lives to Him, for He shall lead you into all Truth and*

# The Children

*Wisdom. In this place where you have wept tears of surrender and sacrifice, I will cause you to reap much joy and you will go forth a holy army unto a dying world. Once you were prisoners; once you were enslaved, but mighty is My Freedom and the harvest from forgiveness.*

*The bitter reaper stands defeated under the Blood, from whence you have continued in all humility. You have chosen well my children - you have chosen mercy and to those who choose mercy, great shall be the mercy that is extended from the Royal Throne. I am here, and My Presence shall not depart from you.*

## Africa

Over the last six years, it's been amazing to pray for Africa as God has led me. Like many others, I long to go there, and be an ambassador for Christ. I was enjoying a restful swim in the local swimming pool when I received this word for Africa. Whilst I was in the water I suddenly I heard a sound in the Spirit of children singing. It was exceptionally loud. I still remember the melody and the drums. I became so engrossed in the vision that I did have to leave the pool eventually. This word will simultaneously bring you great joy and yet will also pierce your heart with compassion for the children of Africa.

## A Wonderful and terrible word for Africa

A Call to Intercede for the Children, in Somalia, Nairobi, and Nigeria. I heard the most glorious sound in the Spirit of thousands of children singing. I could hear African drums playing and the sound lifted me in heavenly joy. The children were singing "Somalia, Somalia, Somalia" and the sound was that of revival. I listened intently, and they sang the names of two other places – "Nairobi, Nairobi and Nigeria, Nigeria". Even as I type this I can hear the sound of their uplifted voices, gloriously in love with Jesus.

The children were lifting the places they were singing of before the throne of God, releasing the will of God on the earth. Their praise was the key that unlocked revival. I was reminded of God's word, that he has ordained praise on the lips of children and infants, because of the enemy and in order to silence the foe and the avenger! (*Psalm 8:2*)

I then saw a vision of the continent of Africa and a huge sickle swung from its northern most tip to its southernmost tip. The sickle signified the beginning of horrific persecution in the places that had been the focus of the songs. I wept as I heard the children continue to sing. Revival could not be stunted, or stopped.

Deep in my spirit, I grieve for those who will give their lives for Christ in Somalia, Nairobi and Nigeria, yet I exalt our heavenly Father for the place of honour amongst the martyrs that they will hold. This is a call for intercessors around the world to link hands in prayer for Africa and the massive revival amongst children that is about to be birthed there. We must pray for this protection and for their faith to be strong.

# CHAPTER 18

# ALL THE YOUNG DUDES

In early 2000 I was busy visiting youth groups around Scotland to try and enlist young people for the 'Take the Land' prayer tour. During one such meeting I met two cool young dudes called Mick and Hugh. I shared a message of repentance with the young people asking them to forgive for the times when they had been wounded or held back by adults. I was sobbing and so was half the hall. Mick and Hugh were part of the 'balling their eyes out brigade' too. We immediately connected, heart to heart, spirit to spirit. It was to be the beginning of the craziest journey together.

Mick and Hugh introduced me to many of their friends and suddenly our home was full of 16-30 year olds. The fridge was continually empty. The phone was constantly ringing. The house was packed, my kids loved it and amidst the chaos God reigned and rocked.

Just when we thought we were heaving at the seams, the Lord delivered a 6' 5" blessing to us in the shape of a passionate 19-year old Canadian Youth for Christ student! Jeremy was working for our church on a year-long project and needed room and board and so, for the next nine months he stayed with us and we learned how to be a family of seven! The friendship was forged in heaven and despite the fact we all occasionally got on one another's nerves (as honest families do), it was glorious and we wouldn't swap a minute of it.

**War room**

In the Summer of 2000 I met with Mick, Hugh and several others to pray about setting up a worship gig where young people could come and lead the praise and the prayer times themselves. We formed a small core team and found a pastor who was willing to let us use his church (thank you David!). I agreed to be alongside the team until they felt confident enough to go it alone. The meetings were billed under this heading, 'no speaker, no agenda, just Jesus'. It was extreme.

Our level of passion freaked out some young people but we were committed to worshipping until breakthrough came. It never looked the same twice. At times breakthrough would come quickly at others times it could take an hour or two before we felt God's presence come as thick as glue – that's when the prophetic songs were released and the dances and the graffiti art and the miracles came. At times all we could do was fall down in the silence in awe of God. Sometimes we wept and screamed our prayers in absolute desperation, convinced God was listening and ready to respond. We even travelled round various parts of Scotland to facilitate the War Room in other churches. It didn't matter if it was five or fifty, the Holy Spirit drew in people who had a heart for this type of encounter with God and many hearts spoke with One voice as the He bound us together.

I think the furthest place to which we travelled was Fraserburgh on the north east coast of Scotland, where we worked with a drug rehabilitation centre for the weekend. Those who travelled in our car were concerned that Mick and I had flipped our lids, because we laughed the entire journey almost without stopping - five and a half hour's worth of side splitting laughter. We needed that laughter to overcome the intense spiritual atmosphere of Fraserburgh, which is a former site of revival in Scotland, but also bears the scars and pain of many church splits and division.

### Prayerstorm

In October 2000 after the Holy Spirit had pounded my head and my heart for several months, I arranged a meeting to explore the possibility of doing a national prayer event with young adults. In response, a handful of young men came from all over Scotland. We squeezed into Stephen's office and prayed and worshipped for around three hours and then we started talking. It was always like that. The business was the worship and out of the worship we did God's business. The Lord gave us Prayerstorm.

Prayerstorm was born from a period of waiting on God, along side young men and women from the emerging generation with a passion for Jesus, and a desire to see a spirit of repentance and brokenness poured out on Scotland. The vision was to 'spark a prayer revolution for revival, releasing the Wind of the Spirit across Scotland'. Our desire was to carry the message of repentance and reconciliation to the youth in our nation and to live the prayer of 2 Chronicles 7:14:

*"If my people who are called by my name, will humble themselves and pray and seek my face, and turn from their wicked ways then I will hear from heaven, I will forgive their sins and I will heal their land."*

When God birthed Prayerstorm in our hearts, we started to meet every Tuesday night to pray and prepare at our house. These meetings continued for about a year even after Prayerstorm had finished. We got some young women on board and the teams began to take shape. We were sending ten teams of twelve to different locations in Scotland. I appointed team leaders for each of the regions we were going to, and the Tuesday night meetings became times of encouragement, training and ministry. My experience as a trainer some years before stood me in good stead for mentoring my young friends. Unexpectedly I found myself leading a group of young adults, who, in turn, would lead others. I didn't have experience of leading other adults but I knew how to follow Jesus and put my trust in Him. Someone once said to me 'Catherine God doesn't call the qualified, He qualifies the called.' I rested in God's faithfulness and prayed for wisdom and compassion to lead like Jesus.

At times there would be around a dozen or so of us but now and then our small lounge would be heaving at the seams with thirty or more twenty somethings. It was hot, crowded, sweaty and glorious. The only down side was that inevitably it was a bit smelly at times with so many bare feet, and the occasional passing of wind (you cannot spend any kind of time around young adults and not experience 'gas emissions' of global concern).

Once we asked the Lord to send his fire, and a thunder and lightning storm broke out across the skyline right there and then, as we prayed. We prayed for hours and the storm kept raging, but we were not afraid. We believed God was totally in the storm. Later on we discovered that another team who were joining us from Raleigh, North Carolina had experienced the exact same phenomenon on the same day that when they also were meeting to pray for Prayerstorm! On another occasion we were praying and worshipping out of the book of Song of Songs. We were utterly captivated by Christ's love for his bride. By the end of the night people were plastered to the floors, the walls and the room was littered with confetti, which I had thrown liberally over everyone!

We invaded each other's lives full on with no compromise and no lies. There wasn't time or space for facades. None of us could be bothered with half-baked holiness. That didn't make us perfect – far from it but - Jesus knew we were earnest in our desire for holy living, even if at times we blew it with our words or actions. We ate together, prayed together, worshipped, socialised, and ministered together. We sometimes even slept together (in separate rooms of course). There was deep mutual respect between us and God honed and shaped the team. I poured myself into my disciples. They meant everything to me and it was a joy to invest in their lives. It was not one-sided. They blessed me more than I think I ever blessed them. They became my dearest friends. To them I was mum, friend, sister, comrade, teacher, confidant and mentor.

### Nameless and faceless on TV

We were working on a low budget, high faith model and didn't have any available funds for marketing and publicising Prayerstorm. We prayed and God intervened giving the mission global coverage without us spending a penny! We were invited to appear on God Channel TV in April of 2001. We walked into the television studios and after a short tour of the building, were instructed to wait there until we were cued. We started praying and couldn't stop. It was a mad Jesus rush as His presence bombarded our weaknesses and covered us in Grace.

In May, UCB Christian Radio station interviewed two of the team via telephone link up, which was another brilliant opportunity to share the vision. We got hooked up with Pete Greig and the 24-7 team and they posted Prayerstorm info on their web site calling youth from the nations to come and join us. We did our part too and drove up and down and around Scotland trying to enlist more Prayerstormers and secure places for teams to stay and to hold meetings. We visited churches and chip shops.

We got stiff limbs from spending hours driving in cars but rejoiced at our divine assignments. We worshipped on trains and streets and anywhere we could lift the name of Jesus. We dared to be different and we didn't care who heard us or what they thought of our unadulterated passion – we just wanted Jesus to love on everyone we met.

Behind the scenes I worked tirelessly at enlisting the backing of various youth organisations, such as Youth for Christ and Youth with a Mission. I attended other leaders meetings and implored the pastors and teachers to get behind this prophetic wave of wonder. I begged prayer leaders to allow us to join their ranks and not to label us as rebels without a cause. Most people were supportive and were willing to make room for something new. I think I was able to convince the majority. God's favour was with us.

We truly were willing to give everything to please Christ. The call to rise up and embrace a new revolution wasn't about rebellion but righteousness. The warfare was for holiness and the lost, the lonely, the dirty and the rejected. It was time to choose whether to be a Nazirite with a circumcised heart for Christ or a Nazi with a heart warped in the barbed wire of hatred and self-importance. We sincerely believed Prayerstorm wasn't just an event, but that it was a slow-burn fuse wire that God would light the furnace of a Jesus revolution in Scotland to mobilise an army of praying, worshipping, prophesying evangelistic young people.

## The Call

I heard about 'The Call' after I read a book by one of my faith 'heroes' Lou Engle. The book was entitled 'Fast Forward' and spoke the same language as me! It was a call to the generations, particularly the youth, to pray and fast and worship. People were meeting in stadiums across America, to petition God for mercy. I was so excited to know that we were part of a global movement that God Himself had initiated. I began to ask the Lord to link Prayerstorm in some way with the Call because the two visions seemed compatible. Within a short time Julie Anderson (Prayer for the Nations and Call UK director) invited me to come to a meeting where she warmly embraced the vision for Prayerstorm and me personally. In July of 2002 I had the privilege of taking a small team of Scottish prayer warriors to the Call England, where we partnered with Julie and Rod and their Call team; we prayed for the UK along with thousands of others. I was blown away to meet Lou Engle and discover he was every bit as humble and passionate for Christ as I had envisaged.

## Stirling Castle

In April, the month before the mission, we went to Stirling and held a prayer and worship concert at the site of the Battle of Stirling and then on into the chapel at the Castle itself. Young men and women led most of the prayer sessions, which were all geared towards repentance for the sins of our nation both past and present.

The Prayerstorm mission was an adventurous project given the short timescale involved and the logistics of moving one hundred and thirty young adults around ten locations simultaneously was not the most straightforward of jobs but we did it thanks to God. I think my children thought mum had had a phone transplant to her ear, since it was almost permanently fixed there for the four weeks before Prayerstorm. I was exhausted by the time the mission arrived but delighted to see the young people take off with their prayers and backpacks full of faith, with more than one hundred of us fasting; we were ready to let God be God.

## Prayerstorm – a holy tornado

In the end people came from Scotland, Canada, Ireland, USA and England. The Holy Spirit endorsed His heart for Scotland, through a sign and wonder in the sky as we headed out of from St Andrew's, our starting point. To our complete amazement a St Andrew's cross was emblazoned across the skyline. The young people left for their prayer assignments with a profound sense of the reality of God going before and with them. We regrouped in Edinburgh our capital city, three days later to hear feedback from each of the teams about how God had moved in their region.

## Comments from team leaders

"In summary I guess it felt like we lived a prayer more than anything. In loving each other whole-heartedly and being committed to love above anything else we discovered a bit of God's heart for Edinburgh. And that was, and is, our prayer.
That we would be so filled with His love as a church that we could truly love Him, truly love each other, and truly love the lost, the broken, the hurting, the poor. And to truly love - what does this look like?? It's not comfortable."

Carla, Edinburgh

"I didn't expect much, but was proven completely wrong - I started crying at the start and still hadn't stopped at the end - with no tissues handy, this was very messy. I just felt the Spirit was there and had broken me and given me a heart for these people."

Steven, St Andrew's

"Various church leaders entered into a time of repentance between the denominations. Nine denominations stood together, holding hands, repenting in a broken and humble way towards each other, asking for forgiveness for their attitude towards each other and for not working together, committing to work together in the future."

Fraser, Inverclyde

"We then visited each of the church buildings in Dumbarton at each site having a short time of repentance and intercession for that particular congregation. During one of these prayer times, a couple of locals with drug problems began to ask us what we were doing. We explained about Prayerstorm and about Jesus. Before we knew it, they had both made commitments to the Lord and asked Him into their hearts. It was amazing that, even though we hadn't come with the intention of evangelism, God still used us to lead these two men to Him."

Matt West Dunbartonshire

"The meeting at Inverness was really encouraging. The highlanders have been given back their voice! It was wonderful to see reconciliation between the generations. This was true and sincere recon-ciliation. It was as though there was a real turning and healing of hearts between the age groups where the young people were being encouraged to run and dream in the Lord standing with the wisdom of the elders."

Howard, North Team Leader

# CHAPTER 19

# REVIVAL

**Revival n.** 1. an improvement in the condition or strength of something  2. an instance of something becoming popular, active, or important again, a re-awakening of religious fervour,
especially by means of evangelistic meetings

**Revivalism n.** 1. belief in or the promotion of a revival of religious fervour. 2. a tendency or desire to revive a formal custom or practise.

### *"O Lord, revive your work" (Habakkuk 3:2)*

I heard the word 'revival' spoken of in Christian circles, but no one ever clearly explained to me what it meant.  I thought about my own spiritual journey.  At fifteen I had passed from death to resurrection life (*Romans 5; Romans 6*) but despite the fact I was a new creation in Christ, my passion for the Lord dwindled over a two-year period and I drifted dangerously away from Jesus.  My wrong choices coupled with catastrophic circumstances almost extinguished my ardour for Christ.  I got tired and zoned out on God and every day I cried a little more and died a little more to my kingdom destiny. On the long road back home to finding God my Father, I experienced a personal spiritual re-awakening.  Sitting in the old church I was overcome with the magnitude of my own sin and paradoxically the immense love of God.  As Amazing Grace poured down on me, the Holy Spirit led me in silent prayers of repentance.  It was so much more than just saying sorry or mere regret or remorse.

In the depths of my being I sorrowed for my sin, acknowledging and confessing it before God.  I had an overwhelming revelation of God's holiness and realised how much my sin had hurt my heavenly Father.  I turned from sin into His loving arms.  Repentance was the key. This opened the floodgates of heaven in my heart at age fifteen, and again at age twenty-nine. I believe mine was a genuine revival, bearing the hallmarks of sincere repentance and lasting conversion. I no longer wanted my old lifestyle.  The reality of my reformation was confirmed by my transformed way of life, and honest desire to labour zealously with God. He took my hard heart and in-grafted His tender and burning love for souls.  Getting back to Jesus was at the core of my revival experience.  I knew before I left the old church that I had been given a fresh start.  My revival was a new beginning of obedience to God. I returned from back sliding into a place of renewed faith.

My revival has been sustained since that time through on-going personal encounters with God flowing out of relationship with Him and obedience to His will and His word. Getting His passion in my heart and in return my heart becoming increasingly more full of His passion for hearts is the DNA in my spiritual genes. I realise now that God longs to revive His sleeping church just as He revived me and yearns to release her to be the miracle working, worshipping, warring Bride He has always intended her to be.

When our holy God draws near during a spiritual re-awakening, people (Christian and non believers alike) become fully conscious of their sinful condition. Deep repentance follows, leading to a breaking down of the heart and a getting down in the dust before God in deep humility. When God visits a person, a town, a city or a nation in such a way, the effect is so wide sweeping that it spills out of the church into the public arena to impact and change the lives of ordinary men, women and children.

God longs to flood the nations with a spirit of repentance. If we will turn from our sins, God will forgive us and heal the land (*2 Chronicles 7:14*). The Word of God clearly teaches us that repentance and revival go hand in hand. We cannot have one without the other. John the Baptist came out of the wilderness saying of Jesus, *'Look, the Lamb of God, who takes away the sin of the world!' John 1:29* Jesus Himself publicly preached the message *'repent for the kingdom of heaven is near Matthew 4:17'*.

Outside the church, there are billions on a path to destruction, who don't even know they need to be revived. All around the world people blaspheme God's name, ignore His commands, commit every sin known under the sun, convince themselves that God doesn't exist, Jesus is just for Christmas, and heaven and hell are make believe. Their hearts are hard, and their eyes are blind, to the reality of God's saving grace.

It is into such a drastic spiritual wilderness that God often pours out His grace and mercy through a sovereign visitation of His presence and power in revival. It is frequently the most hardened of criminals, drunkards, and prostitutes who abandon themselves fully to Christ.

### Wales

I picked up some church history books and began to study the history of Church revival. I was amazed to discover that in 1904 God's Spirit broke out all across Wales, using a young Welsh man named Evan Roberts as a lightning rod for this movement. Such was the transforming effect of the Holy Spirit on the entire nation that whole football stadiums were emptied. It was known as the 'white glove' revival because the crime rate almost entirely disappeared and the police had no criminals to deal with!

## Scotland

My heart was stirred as I read of the incredible awakening in Scotland during the 1939 and 1949 revivals on the island of Lewis where Rev Duncan Campbell and several others preached uncompromisingly, on the Gospel of grace, love and holiness. A handful of faithful people had prayed in an old barn for several months before the outpouring. They entered into covenant with the Lord and prayed until He visited the island with a mighty move of His Spirit, which brought people out of the pubs, the dance halls and their homes onto the streets and up to the church steps where they cried out asking 'how can we be saved?' as they wept under conviction of sin.

## Ireland

Tears of joy and expectation ran down my cheeks as details of the Irish revival in 1859-63 unfolded in my studies. During this outpouring school children were deeply affected by the Holy Spirit and children were reportedly seen crying out to God for forgiveness in their classrooms and leading each other in prayers of salvation. When parents arrived to collect their children from the school in Colerain, they were converted on the spot and ministers were sent for, to help with counselling.

This Irish revival apparently had its beginnings in a New York prayer meeting, which was started by Jeremiah Lamphier in 1847. It spread across North America, sweeping an estimated one million converts into God's Kingdom and crossed the Atlantic into Ulster early in 1859. The remainder of the UK was impacted later in the year, also resulting in a million conversions. ('Children in Revival, Kingdom Kids, Harry Sprange)

## Heroes of the faith in every continent

I was captivated by the passion of the Englishmen John Wesley and George Whitefield whom God used to birth the Methodist movement and to save countless souls through their fearless preaching during the 18th century awakening. George Whitefield apparently agonised in bed for seven weeks before finally receiving salvation. Wesley, born in 1703, the 15th of nineteen children, narrowly escaped with his life after a fire destroyed his father's rectory at the age of six. Charles Finney, born the year after Wesley died, who caused uproar with his powerful message of holiness, and wherever he went there was either revival or riots astonished me! Through his preaching more than half a million converts were won for Christ. I marvelled at stories of Dwight L Moody, the shoe salesman from Boston who got saved in a shoe shop, poured himself into Sunday school work, gave up his job at 24 years of age to enter full time ministry, and went on to become one of the world's greatest evangelists.

I've always loved the song 'Amazing Grace' and I thought Grace even more amazing when I discovered John Newton had written it. John was born in 1725 and by his early twenties was a slave trader and a blasphemer who lived a life of debauchery. For years he was only half convinced that the Scriptures were true but ultimately he believed Jesus was the only Mediator who could save him from his sins and God's holy wrath. It was during a violent Atlantic storm he had a profound experience, which led to him becoming a preacher and prolific hymn writer, and for the rest of his life he campaigned tirelessly for the abolition of slavery.

I was both humbled and slightly terrified by the antics of a Yorkshire plumber named Smith Wigglesworth, born in 1859. His motto was 'only believe' and he hated sickness with such a passion that he would violently attack it, often punching a sick person, striking the relevant ailing body party with extreme force. He was uneducated and a straight talking man who helped fire the growing worldwide Pentecostal movement. He was a fearless pioneer and healer. He rocked churches out of their comfort zone. He was gruff, tough and abrupt and the devil was his number one enemy. He was like a boxer in the spirit, literally punching the sickness right out of people! Smith Wiggelsworth loved the Holy Spirit with all of his heart.

Many other great men and women of faith stood out from the pages of history to me. Just a few of the others who impacted my life include the great Irish Saint Patrick; Martin Luther, whose watchword was 'by faith alone'. John Knox, the great Scottish reformer; Charles H Spurgeon, a gifted preacher and evangelist from the Baptist movement still considered today to be one of the greatest Christian teachers of all time. Amy Carmichael, the Irish lass from County Down, who found her life's work in India, where she became a Christian missionary to the temple children; David Livingston, the mill boy from Blantyre who served as a doctor missionary in Africa for 33 years; Mary Slessor, inspired by her hero David Livingstone, left for Africa just two years after David's death, and spent the rest of life working there as a missionary.

William J Seymour, the son of ex-slaves, and Frank Bartleman, who turned a stable on Azusa Street, Los Angeles into a hub of revival; William and Catherine Booth, founders of the Salvation

Army, took to the streets to demonstrate the love of Christ with actions and words.  Kathryn Kuhlman, who won the hearts of many sceptics and whose miracle meetings saw thousands saved, healed and delivered; J Hudson Taylor and C T Studd, both missionaries to China who refused to count the cost of loving Christ and would not turn back from the path they had chosen.  Studd's words challenged me deeply, 'some wish to live within the sound of Church or Chapel bell; I want to run a Rescue shop with a yard of hell.'

Down through the ages every continent has experienced some form of spiritual awakening. From the great African church father Augustine, come words of incalculable wisdom in the opening prayer of his Confessions, 'our hearts are restless until they can find peace in You.'

## Salvations and healings

Reading about men and women of faith that God had used to usher in revivals of salvations, healings and miracles created a deep hunger in me to serve Jesus in a similar manner.  I took my first tentative steps at prayers for healing in 1996 when I was baptised in the Spirit and an elderly lady was healed at the same time.  That very night I felt the fire of God course through my hands and it ignited a desire to pray for the sick that has never left me. In 1997 I prayed with my friend Robert for healing from cancer, but he passed away only a few weeks later.  In 1998, after my mum suffered a massive heart attack I prayed for her too, but she died within forty-eight hours.

After several apparent 'failures' I was afraid to pray for sick people for a while but then the urge to love compelled me to get back on my knees and back into action in prayers for healing.  I prayed for a man in church with a migraine and he was healed instantly.  I prayed for a lady's knee and as I placed my hand on her leg, her knee-cap began to vibrate noisily.  I didn't know what to say or do but when I had finished praying, she exclaimed loudly 'what was that'? I told her it was God at work. The woman was not a Christian and marvelled at the Lord's restorative work on her shattered bone pieces.

I began to receive reports of wonderful healing testimonies about a young Canadian evangelist named Todd Bentley who was being used by God to heal people in their hundreds from every kind of conceivable disease and sickness. I was enthralled with the healing power of Jesus and I begged Him to send Todd to Scotland. He did! I organised a small speaking tour for Todd and he ministered in several places around Scotland in the spring of 2001.  I stepped into a new level of faith being around him!  Todd regularly receives words of knowledge about the conditions of sick people who attend the healing meetings at which he is present. I decided to ask Jesus to use me in the same way. I frequently receive words of knowledge about emotional or spiritual wounds but until this point I had rarely stepped out in faith for words of knowledge about physical sickness.

In preparation for the meeting with Todd, I was astounded when God gave me a list of ailments that people were suffering from! I experienced a pain in my womb and the Spirit shared with me that several women had conditions of sickness relating to their wombs or ovaries; this pain left me and then I felt a pain in my back, the Spirit told me that someone was coming to the meeting with a serious back problem. On and on the list went. I wrote them all down and set off for Stirling to rendezvous with Todd. The pain did not persist. God had used my body only momentarily as a prayer prompt.

At the healing meeting Todd preached and then we entered in to a time of ministry. I also shared what the Lord had given me and all but one of the conditions I had prayed about came forward for prayer! People were falling all over the place as the power of God hit the meeting like a tornado.

Over the last three years I have continued to step out in faith on many occasions for people asking for prayer ministry. I have seen people gloriously delivered from demons and sickness. I have seen a couple of people receive partial healing from deafness but although I have prayed for blind eyes, I have not yet witnessed them healed. I have prayed for paralysed people and many kinds of physical ailments. I once was so full of faith that I lifted a grown man out of his wheelchair and held him for five minutes single-handed whilst praying for his healing. Being able to hold him on my own was a miracle in itself. I was desperate for the man to be healed but he did not walk. On another occasion it was my joy to observe an elderly lady throw away her walking stick and run round the room after Jesus healed her foot.

### Jesus my healer

I had been in a considerable amount of pain for some time and decided to seek medical advice. During a routine smear examination in 2001 the doctor discovered I had a large lump on the left side of my womb. She referred me to a specialist for a scan and whatever follow up treatment might be necessary. I was not having it! I laid hands on myself and told the lump to go away in Jesus name. Stephen prayed for me, as did my friend Hugh Black. When I attended my appointment, the scan operator enquired why I had come. She looked at my notes perplexed and said, 'according to these you have a large lump on the left side of your womb, but I can't see anything; you are totally fine.' I smiled at her and said God had healed me.

**Why?**

I have a chronic back problem. Some days I weep with fatigue and the constant barrage of pain. For the most part, the only time I am totally pain free is when I minister under the anointing of the Holy Spirit. I never feel pain when I am preaching, teaching, prophesying, witnessing or praying with others! It is a choice I make in love to drive long distances to minister or type for long hours to prepare teaching notes etc. It is not always easy but it is another aspect of worshipping Jesus with my life.

With each pregnancy my spine, pelvis and neck bones and ligaments have become weaker and weaker. I have received much prayer for healing and at times the Lord has delivered me from agonising pain. However, the delivery has not been permanent. I believe God wants to heal me and is able to heal me. One day I asked my friend Hugh why he thought I wasn't being healed? He answered me in his usual quiet and wise way. He said "Catherine, there was an unanswered 'why' on the Cross," *'Eloi, Eloi, lama sabachtani? Which means, My God, my God, why have you forsaken me?' Matthew 27:46.* Hugh went on to remind me that Jesus Himself died with an unhealed body before being fully and completely restored to His Father upon resurrection. He said to me, 'child if the Lord heals you it is for His glory and if, for whatever reason He does not heal you, then it is also for His glory.' I pondered those thoughts and thanked Jesus for being my strength when all I felt was weak. His grace is sufficient for our needs.

Everywhere I preach I try to pray for the sick but not everyone gets healed. I don't pretend to understand why, but I am convinced that God does something wonderful under the anointing of the Holy Spirit every time we pray in faith, even if we cannot see the effect with our physical eyes, or the answer to our prayer looks different to what we had anticipated. I recall one elderly lady asking me to pray for her just as I was leaving a meeting. I was exhausted and really wanted to go home after ministering for around five hours. I looked at her feet and they were twisted and warped, her legs were covered in cists. The poor woman was in agony. I felt waves of compassion welling up in me, and I got to me knees and laid hands on her feet and prayed with every ounce of faith in me. I wept over those dear feet and kissed them as I prayed. I quietly begged Jesus to heal them. They weren't healed but the most beautiful thing happened. The old lady looked at me and smiled. She helped me to my feet and then giggling, said she felt like dancing! Her feet remained gnarled but during that prayer the Lord healed her heart and she regained her joy. She told me she had never felt happier, and it didn't matter about her feet! His ways are not our ways and His thoughts are not our thoughts.

I believe that one day the banks of healing will burst in the ministry the Lord has entrusted to me and I am surely going to keep praying for the sick until the Lord calls me home. In the meantime I will continue to pray for the sick and for those others who minister in gatherings of thousands and observe revival power flowing.

## Salvations

I fast for souls to be saved, but have not yet personally witnessed large numbers of people coming to Christ. However, it's been awesome to see the first fruits of salvations of people I know and love and from strangers too. Every single soul matters to Jesus. My children Mark, Daniel and Rebecca were three of the first people I prayed through to conversion. Samuel has not prayed the 'sinner's prayer' but has a profound connection with Jesus. I started praying for a friend of mine twenty-two years ago just after I became a Christian at age fifteen. She received her salvation in 2002 and I jumped for joy and screamed with delight for two whole hours when she told me Jesus was her Lord and Saviour! I prayed for my mum for years too, and believe with all my heart that she went home to be with the Lord when she died in 1998.

I prayed with Robert, my friend with cancer, and he was saved. I continue to intercede for my family and friends who do not yet know Jesus. I've been praying for some people I know for more than twenty years. I won't give up, although at times I may feel like it. Perseverance is a priceless pearl in the kingdom. I cannot boast of huge numbers of conversions that I know of, but I have sown seed for souls for many years. We have to keep pushing in prayer together and believe that the Holy Spirit will march our family and friends out of the jaws of hell and into the arms of our Heavenly Father.

## Prophetic Evangelism

After preaching sermons to my home walls for a couple of years, God released me on the unsuspecting public. I only began preaching three years ago and during that time I've learned how to get the butterflies in my stomach to fly in formation and to overcome feelings of nausea and rely on the Holy Spirit for strength and inspiration. I have battled with physical frailties and perceived spiritual ones. Initially I didn't think I was qualified to preach and I seriously considered enrolling at University to do a theology degree. I didn't feel the Lord was really asking me to do that, but I thought people might take me more seriously if I had letters after my name!

God spoke to me from His word and as I read of Peter and John and their mighty exploits in the book of Acts, I was convinced that if God could use *'unschooled ordinary men'* (*Acts 4:13*) like these to His glory, He could use me too,without a diploma or degree. I poured myself into reading God's word and I was delighted when I preached for the first time without notes last year! I've come a long way, and the further I come, the more I realise I have much to learn. My heart's cry remains, 'Lord don't let me harm the Body'. Regardless of age, background, creed, colour or gender, the preaching path I am travelling along is also open to all who will respond to God's invitation to share His word.

Sometimes when I preach the Lord will release personal prophetic words to those who are gathered in the meeting. At other times there will not be any personal prophecies, but the sermon itself will be the prophetic message from the Lord to a particular church or nation. I have never preached the same sermon twice (yet!) because I believe the Lord has something new to say in every situation and circumstance. I've stepped out in faith and delivered teaching, facilitated workshops and different styles of sermons to all different types of people in many situations, denominations, fellowships, halls and the streets too! I've preached to churches of just a handful of people, travelling a four hour round trip to be with them and latterly to a gathering of around one thousand in Ireland. The numbers don't matter; it's following Jesus that counts. I've preached for love and sometimes I've received gifts. At other times, people haven't been able to offer anything except a 'thank you', and that's ok. The greatest blessing is to bring joy to my Father through obedience and surrender.

During the last two years I have experienced the phenomenon of seeing non-Christians give their lives to Christ in meetings, through the prophetic ministry. On one such occasion I was ministering in Stirling and a young lady caught my attention at the back of the meeting hall. The Lord released a powerful word over her life. All I remember of the word was the final line, 'don't miss the day of His visitation'. I didn't realise she wasn't a Christian until the pastor introduced me to her later in the evening, sharing with me that the teenager had just given her heart to Christ as a direct result of the prophecy. This has happened a number of times now in meetings. It's wonderful and exciting to witness the fruit of salvation from prophetic evangelism. Just like preaching, prophecy is another divine opportunity for all Spirit filled believers to partner the God of miracles.

I've also received words of knowledge in every day walks of life. Once, I was having my hair coloured at the hairdresser's. I was dripping with bleach when I had a vision of the junior stylist. In the vision, she was a little girl and was attempting to drink a glass of water, but choked in the process. I shared the picture with her on a prompt from the Lord. It turned out the girl had a fear of drinking water and couldn't take a drop without coughing violently. I offered to pray with her, but she declined. However, each time we meet she remembers the prayer picture and draws a little closer to her Heavenly Father. That's what it's all about – bringing people into relationships with Jesus.

# CHAPTER 20

## THE COMMISSION

**Commission n.** 1. an instruction or command. > an order for something, especially a work of at, to be produced specially. > archaic, the authority to perform a task. 2. a group of people 3. given official authority to do something . 4. a warrant conferring the rank of military officer.

One of the many books I read about revival was by a man named Hugh Black, the co-founder of Struthers Memorial churches in Scotland. Hugh spent a considerable amount of time ministering with Rev Duncan Campbell in the Lewis revivals and his writings and testimonies are full of wisdom and Godly insights. After reading 'Living in the Reality of Revival' I turned to the final page of the book and noticed there was an address and telephone contact number for Mr Black. I was astonished that it was only about 20 miles from my home.

I clearly heard the Holy Spirit tell me to contact Mr Black and ask if he would meet with me with the express purpose of commissioning me for the Take the Land prayer tour. I was extremely nervous about calling a stranger especially someone whom I respected as a leader in the Body of Christ, but with shaking hand I dialled the number. Mr Black wasn't home but his wife was very kind to me and took my telephone number and asked 'have you experienced the baptism of the Spirit my dear?' I was delighted to be able to tell her that I had.

Mr Black did return my call and agreed to meet with me. In early 2000 I met with Hugh and was both terrified and excited to spend time talking with him. He had a lovely sense of humour and it was such a joy to sit and listen to his stories and testimonies. We became firm friends and Mr Black became a spiritual father to me. I had many teachers in my life prior to this, but never a father. It was a priceless gift from Jesus.

Mr Black did go on to commission me for the work Christ had set before me. Although I had good accountability relationships with others at this time, I believed Mr Black was to specifically release me for the Take the land Prayer tour. He agreed. He laid hands on me and sent me off with Father's blessing and his personal endorsement.

The Lord called Hugh home in the spring of 2001. I still miss him greatly but I cherish his input into my life for those eighteen months. Hugh was respected by people from every walk of life and was held in high esteem by leaders from many nations. Amongst his many graces and gifts he was known for his humility and profound love of Christ; he was a fearless pioneer for Pentecost and the baptism of the Holy Spirit as well as leading the way for women to minister as co-equals in Christ.

This book is also Father's blessing and commissioning to the many thousands who will read it and respond to their call in Christ. Your journey doesn't have to look like mine but by sharing real life I believe we can spur each other on to greater works of faith and bring glory to Jesus name. I believe every single man, woman and a child has a unique calling and destiny in Christ that no other can fulfil. You were created for His glory, for adventures, for suffering and untold joy.

If telling my story even in some tiny way helps to release **YOU** to run with your God-given visions and your passion then every tear-stained page I've written and each lesson I have learned has been worth it! If people don't know what your passion is you haven't got one. If Christ is your obsession run with the call He has placed on your life without fear, shame or intimidation, but whatever you do, run into Jesus not works. It's all about relationship with Him.

Perhaps you are hurting and this book has triggered some points for prayer? Take heart and pursue your healing for all you are worth and don't give up and give in to the devil. Satan loves to kick us when we are down, so why not kick back and hold out for the Healer? Maybe you like my story but don't feel as though your life can ever change? Don't despair; your life in Jesus makes a difference. Receive His Truth and believe it. Or perhaps you are already fired up and ready to run to the nations? Well go for it and when you fall down don't count it as defeat. Just get back on your feet and keep on running with the Wind of the Spirit. The Lord will bless your radical obedience.

If you don't know your calling don't be phased by that just meditate on this – the need is the call. Respond to the need that you see all around you. People don't care how much you know until they know how much you care. If you want to see something new, do something new, but do it for Jesus. Life is not about what you accomplish; it's about what God sets in motion through you. Two thousand years ago Jesus put salvation in motion and He is still in the business of transforming individuals and nations. His Holy principles transcend culture, countries and all communication. Revival comes from being in His presence. You've been revived with His life giving Breath and words, now go and preach the gospel, resurrect the dead, deliver the oppressed, cleanse the lepers and heal the sick. You were born to be a miracle now **GO** and let a miracle be born

### The wind of the spirit is blowing

*"I looked, and I saw a windstorm coming out of the north – an immense cloud with flashing lightning and surrounded by brilliant light … Like the appearance of a rainbow in the clouds on a rainy day, so was the radiance around him. This was the appearance of the likeness of the glory of the Lord. When I saw it, I fell facedown, and I heard the voice of one speaking."*

Ezekiel 1:25-28

I heard the sound of a mighty Wind blowing in the heavens. It was so loud I covered my ears. I shouted, 'Lord, what is it?"

He replied, *"Child, it is the Wind of my Spirit blowing across the nations. Tell My children to get in the Wind".*

The weight of God's presence impacted me like an atomic bomb and in an instant I knew a deeper reverence of Jesus than I have ever known before. I trembled and shook in awe before God who created the dawn and stretched out the heavens in His mighty hands. Despite the deafening sound of the Wind, I was safe in Jesus' arms. Intimacy with Christ is a sure shelter from the storms that rage around us.

God is One God in Three Divine Persons – Father, Son and Holy Spirit. Throughout history, God the Spirit has revealed Father and Jesus in a multitude of different ways to His people. At times He uses the elements of creation to speak to those He created. Fire, wind, water, cloud and earthquakes have been utilised by God to demonstrate His presence and power.

In Moses' day the Spirit revealed to the Israelites that God was with them through a pillar of cloud by day and fire by night *(Ex 13:21-22)*. When God needed to convince Elijah of His great majesty, He split the rocks with a wind, an earthquake and then fire, finally speaking to the trembling prophet in a whisper *(1 Kings 19:9-18)*. The prophet Ezekiel was caught up in the company of the living Lord when a holy Wind lifted the prophet into God's glory *(Ezekiel 1)*. When the church was born at Pentecost, *'suddenly a sound like the blowing of a violent wind came and filled the whole house where they were sitting' (Acts 2:2)*

**When a Holy Wind starts to blow, God's people need to listen to what he is saying!**

**God is the Wind** – One name for the Holy Spirit is 'ruach'. It means breath or wind. This Wind represents the moving of the Holy

## The Commission

Spirit on, in, over and through the lives of individuals, churches, people groups and ultimately whole nations. When God is in the Wind, it contains his glory and every aspect of his divine nature and character. It is full of his Holiness, Righteousness, Mercy, Compassion, Wisdom, Grace, Purity, Love and Power.

**Wind separates wheat from chaff – surrender to the sifting!** This Holy Wind will direct believers towards purity and away from the ways of the world. We will experience a sifting in our hearts and respond to the call to be set apart for Christ. Wind and fire often go hand in hand and as we are cleansed by the Holy Spirit He will rekindle passion in our hearts for our First Love Jesus. *Matthew 3:11b, 12*

**This wind of the Holy Spirit will turn the nations back to God and the generations to each other**, in like manner to Elijah the prophet (*1 Kings 18:37*). The Lord will confront the Bride of her worldliness; compromise and lack of holiness i.e. reveal our sinful condition!

**A fresh breath of power evangelism will break out in the nations** (*Acts 2:40, 41*) Power evangelism is simply Jesus being Jesus through his disciples as signs and miracles accompany the preaching of the gospel message.

### Breaking news

Don't get freaked out by the extremes of weather and the outbreak of wars. God is in contol. In the face of what we see with our human eye, we trust in him and his plan with the eye of faith and trust his word.

*'When you hear of wars and revolutions, do not be frightened. These things must happen first, but the end will not come right away ... there will be great earthquakes, famines and pestilence in various places, and fearful events and great signs from heaven.' Luke 20:9,11*

**The nameless and faceless** will come out of the wilderness looking like Jesus and produce good fruit. Many prodigals will reject the world and return to their Heavenly Father's loving embrace. Reverence for God will increase, as people comprehend that he is holy, just and compassionate.

The Elisha (double portion) generation will be come forward in this next move of the Spirit. A holiness movement will break out amongst the older generations who in turn will influence the emerging generations as spiritual mothers and fathers.

**The Holy Spirit will restore the fallen, the flunked out and the failing of God's army.** Many have become barren and have fallen into spiritual stupor through exhaustion, discouragement, depression, despair, weariness, loss of vision and hopelessness. This refreshing and healing will raise those with religious rigor mortis to be an army of resurrected Holy Spirit warriors.

*"Prophesy to these bones and say to them, 'Dry bones, hear the word of the Lord! This is what the Sovereign Lord says to these bones: I will make breath (wind or Spirit) enter you, and you will come to life . . . So I prophesied as he commanded me, and breath entered them; they came to life and stood up on their feet – a vast army." Ezekiel 37:4-10*

**Wind brings movement and movement brings change. Get ready to go!** When God is on the move by his Spirit he brings us out of captivity, away from passivity and into stability. He is then able to position his people where he wants them to be. Initially, change can make us feel uncomfortable - this is God's way of getting us to rely on him and not on our own strength.

**Ignore introspection and reject rejection** - the devil will resist and oppose this move of God through hardships and hostility. Our call is to persevere, ignore Satan's distractions and continue to hope in God.

**Calling all Watchmen** - the Wind of the Spirit will release many to become watchmen (those who will stand and watch in prayer) for their nations with a fresh zeal and passion for 24-hour intercession. Ezekiel got caught up in a Windstorm of God's glory and was sent out to Israel as God's spokesperson. *Ezekiel 3:16,17*

**Watchers stand on Walls** - just like Ezekiel, many more watch men and women will be raised up to pray for the land and the people of Israel. Jewish believers are uniquely positioned in God to prophesy to the Breath.

*"I have posted watchmen on your walls, O Jerusalem; they will never be silent day or night. You who call on the Lord, give yourselves no rest, and give him no rest till established Jerusalem and makes her the praise of the earth." Isaiah 62:6,7*

# The Commission
## There is glory in the wind

*"This was the appearance of the likeness of the glory of the Lord. When I saw it, I fell facedown, and I heard the voice of one speaking." Ezekiel 1:28b*

It is time for the Windstorm of his Presence to break out in the nations. Many will see and experience the Glory of God in the same way as Ezekiel, who heard the Spirit then saw the blazing beauty of Almighty God. God's glory is going to increase on the earth as we seek His face.

Winds can bring blessing but they can also cause desolation and destruction. Ultimately, the Holy Spirit will release the holy and righteous judgements of God upon the nations. Those who respond to God in humility and obedience will know the inexpressible depths of resurrection forgiveness and grace.

The Gospel will be preached in power to every tribe and nation on earth, before the great and terrible day of the Second Coming of our Lord Jesus Christ (Revelation 19, 20, 21) Beloved, the Lord is saying, ***"Get in the Wind"***. Let it carry you into His higher purposes.

The Wind of the Warrior, Christ Jesus the Deliverer, is blowing! It is an equipping, sanctifying, consecrating, dead raising, and God-glorifying, Wind of Deliverance and Life!

Amen

Further copies available from

In the UK:

Gatekeepers
18 Castle View
West Kilbride
Ayrshire KA23 9HD
Scotland
UK

01 294 823926

Bulk order discount e-mail: insomnia@yerton.com


In the US:

Just Publishing
408 Pacific Oaks Road
Goleta, CA, 93117
USA


Bulk order discount email: jpdi@runbox.com


If you have encountered God in a fresh way, or received
encouragement from this book, we would love to hear from you.

Email Catherine at: <u>Catherine@gatekeepers.org.uk</u>

Email Just Publishing at: <u>jpdi@runbox.com</u>

## About the Author

Catherine Brown, (38) is married to Stephen (39) and they have four children Mark (13), Daniel (8), Rebecca (7) and Samuel (3). The family stay in a beautiful village on the West coast of Scotland, where Stephen runs the family business.